A Fleeting Presence

fieldnotes from a crone

Reader's Comments

Your writing continues to ferment and mature, packing more and more of a wallop with each draught. *Messages from the Neolithic* was an uplifting affirmation for me: To read about this way of being in the world, articulated as verifiably real and not pointlessly delusional, snapped me back into the truth of my own lived experience and gives me courage to continue on my path.

—WILL C. TUCSON, AZ

I loved *Immense Continuity*! I definitely resonate with this as I think about praising slowness and the loss of so many skill sets being filled by computers or screen time.

—BETH F. RIMROCK, AZ

You are such a gifted writer! I love reading your words.

—VIDYA M. SALIDA, CO

Thank you for sharing your writing. I find it brilliant and evocative.

—WINDEAGLE K. ABIQUIU, NM

I read the title of your article and thought I'd read a little way into the first paragraph. Too late! I read every word to the end. Every evocative word. You're a brilliant writer. I got whiffs of heather and burning peat and felt a sea breeze.

—BILL K. DENVER, CO

This is so, so in tune with who I am, where I come from, what I am trying to discover and heal inside of me. Beautiful work, beautiful words. Different part of the world, different culture, but same story. Thank you for bringing these things closer to the surface for me!

—KAT S. HERNANDEZ, NM

A Fleeting Presence

fieldnotes from a crone

SUSAN CROSS

Published by Madrona Arts Press
ISBN (Paperback): 978-1-7327890-2-9
ISBN (ebook): 978-1-7327890-3-6
Illustrations: Susan Cross
Cover: Susan Cross
Author photo: Vidya McClutchey

Printed in the United States of America

About the Crone

The Crone, with her many names—Kali, Skeleton Woman, La Loba, the Cailleach, Lady Death, the Morrigan, the Hag—is the master of the Life/Death/Life cycle.

In modern usage, "crone" is most often considered a pejorative. For most of us the word crone conjures up images of a withered old woman, a black-clad witch, or a ragged hag. That this characterization is what so readily comes to mind demonstrates the success of those who have worked for centuries to discredit and vilify the crone aspect of the goddess.

The Crone archetype, followed back through history to the farthest reaches that can be documented, seems to have symbolized an embodiment of the deep creative void of nature. The Crone was the One that existed before all creation and by whom all creation will be absorbed in the end. The goddess in her triple aspect was the seat of creative power, was the water, the earth, the landscape, providence, the mother of animals, of everything. She gave and took away in great cycles of birth, life, and death.

The humans who were steeped in Mother Goddess symbology were grounded in, and intimately bound, to the gritty daily realities of life and death. They experienced the annual cycling of the visible world through plants, animals, and skies, and had a clear-cut connection to seasonal fluxes. They were intimately in touch with the births and deaths of family and clan. They were in touch with the natural world in a way we can only imagine.

Much of our knowledge of the life/death/life cycle is contaminated by our culture's fear of death. Therefore, our abilities to move through cycles of this type are frail and stunted.

The Crone is always old, the Grandmother, the Wise Woman, carrier of female wisdom, and giver of council that is clear and clean. The crone's ability to advise is gained by long personal life experience but is not contaminated with personal agendas. She is elementally neutral yet caring.

Praise Poem for the Crone

I am of many names.
At the dark of the year I become Crone of Ancestral Memory.

I am older than language,
older than the circles of stone,
older than the rotation of the stars around Polaris.

I come from the void.
I come from nothingness into form.
I set out the mountains and
caused the rivers between them to flow.
The loom of life is mine, warp and weft.
I spin the yarn of time.

My beauty is darkness,
like still deep water under a moonless sky.
My eye reflects starlight—small glinting sparks of silver.

When you look at clean bone, you see me.
When you watch cold water wear away stone, you see me.

Come beside me.
I offer silence, rest, and transformation.

I sing in the interstices of cricket calls and raven caws.
I sing the softness of waiting, the quiet of watching,
I am the hush of the mound.

I live in the depths of the Earth.
The holy springs rise from my dwelling.
I reside below the bear's den,
beneath the badger's lair,
under the bottomless cave.

I drink the icy air of pure intelligence,
am sustained by the fire of the heart.
My fodder is polarity and unity.
I consume opposites and emit wholeness.

Order and chaos flow from me.
The great cycles, the moving seasons, the phases of the moon.
I am the rise and fall of the wave,
the potential of the seed,
the crumbling of the bone.

People fear me yet rest unaware in my embrace.
Most resist me,
but the wise are conscious of my web.
I am the giver of apt limits and of will.
Harmony and balance gentle me.
Excess inflames my fierceness.

With or without you I live on.
In the vastness of the stellar reaches I spin on.
In the single cell I replicate myself.
In the molten stone at the core of the Earth I move.
I stir the waters.
I breathe the clouds.
With or without you.
I live on.

The Curriculum of the Crone

These fieldnotes are an offering, a kind of gift. But gifts such as this ask something in return. Like for like. Here are the shiny mica particles, pottery sherds, owl feathers, bones, herbs, and arcane symbols scratched on stone. They are laid out on mats woven of wool, and linen, and nettle, like on a market day. As you watch, I assemble things, wrap them like a shydi, a medicine bundle. I make eye contact with you as I pass it to your palm, sincere, reticent, trusting. Carried in that speaking look, there's a hoped-for energetic reciprocity, a hoped-for receptivity, a gentle faith in being met and held.

These fieldnotes ask something of you, as they've asked something of me. Attention, pondering, work. They ask you to witness the on-going evolution of one old woman, an every-woman, a crone remembering, a crone learning. As you read, you witness an individual into being. This attesting is necessary for our existence, for staying human. I give freely what little I've gathered, absorbed, and discovered. My gratitude for your consideration is great.

This set of writings and sketches explores the Curriculum of the Crone through a very personal lens: ancestors, death, dissolution, and pilgrimage. The products of the Crone's "caldron of transformation" are not unpromising or gloomy. In the shadowy places lie fulcrums, watershed ridges, seeds, growth, and needed change. From Her deep place, we witness the elegant arc of the whole cycle, feel the gravitational pull of reality, sense the unending repetition of life/death/ life and grasp the smallness of our individual moment on this miraculous Earth.

This slim book is for anyone who is growing older each day, for those who have ancestors, for those who will die, for people who have had their life explode in surprising ways, and for those who seek.

With Great Love,
Susan Cross
Abiquiu, New Mexico Fall 2020

Contents

Ancestors

1

Hidden

Where do you begin with such a thing? When you tug on any ragged thread the pull is felt five hundred years back, a thousand years back, perhaps clear to ten thousand years ago, to the Neolithic Revolution.

You tug and a weak flame flickers to life in a damp dark place. Your ancestor's bones begin to ache. Your own bones begin to ache. Your heart aches. You start to comprehend that your tendency toward appeasement, invisibility, and self-editing is causally related to their survival mechanisms. *Oh.*

It's an epigenetic homeopathic dilution. For your people there was true and present danger; genocide, oppression, burnings, beatings, famine—and for you, epigenetic switches are clicked on for anxiety, fat storage, wariness. *Oh.*

This narrative has come to me in bits and pieces over an extended arc of time. Like a whiff of peat smoke on a breeze or an evil feeling in a churchyard, little clues have been accumulating since childhood. Fragments of my mother's superstitions resolve into Irish diaspora tales. *They came from Connacht. Oh.* Things I have a deep affinity for, like rugged coastlines and lapstrake rowing boats turn out to be "heritage" not just some strange preference. *They came from Kilbrandon and Kilchattan. Oh.* The sensation is of a slow-motion puzzle clacking together.

In my youth, there was no deliberate transference of heritage. No cultural underpinnings. No creaky relatives leaning on a cane and telling me legends of the home country. In fact, there was deliberate severance. A leaving behind of the unpleasant memories of political upheaval and personal trauma. An American reset, a new beginning, a fresh place with possibility. A great forgetting.

Yet we and the ancestors are linked in oddly hinged ways. Lineage mycelia runs through the ether. Ancestral telluric currents wait for amplification. The relatedness doesn't go away even if we wish it. It's subtle. It's mysterious. Our ancestors, even if neglected for ten thousand years, are still an on-going part of our current manifestation. They bore us. We carry them.

We carry their strengths and their weaknesses. They are reservoirs of potential great gifts; perseverance, courage, steadfastness, humor, valor, cunning, rootedness, skill, heredity. We are also tainted by their famines, silenced by their land clearances. We are the children of the children of those who had to hide well and stay hidden. We are the children of the children of those who endured shattered and oppressed cultures, forbidden languages, demonized ways.

When you begin excavating the stories and experiences of your ancestors you may churn up fear or shame or a strange sense of having betrayed them by exposing their techniques for survival. *We still aren't safe—you aren't safe—what are you doing?!* You may be rattled by the bone-deep, soul-deep loneliness you feel. Your own newly exposed hiddennesses and lack of belonging may make of you a sorrowing pilgrim. You may find yourself traipsing through the long-term ramifications of racism, colonialism, and religious oppression.

We can begin to understand then, at some unconscious soul level, the on-going sensations we feel of the dangers of speaking up and being noticed. We can sense in our own bodies the instinctive fear of powerful men with governments behind them. Our hearts can atavistically suffer the inconceivable loss of traditional music, ritual, stories, and healing ways. Like echoes, history repeating itself, we jointly face the betrayals of those we thought we could trust. *We carry them. The same things are with us now in different forms.*

They want to help us. They want to be known and remembered. We want to belong. To have continuity. Borne together, us and them, swept along on the archaic whisper, we recognize a shared deep longing for a reality that once was. A whole culture, a home landscape, being claimed by a people and a place. Often flawed and imperfect, yes. But intact. We desperately want to belong to something unshattered, unashamed, sound, whole.

It's a peculiarly North American affliction, this longing for continuity, community, and tradition. A nation of amputated exiles and cultural orphans, we find ourselves severed, displaced, and yearning for legacy and place at the same time we hold a great distain for this very thing. The stifled desires come out twisted, as our youth culture, materialism, in individualism and the cult of personality, in our constant need for movement and novelty, in our tendency toward cultural appropriation.

I'm a third-generation daughter of diaspora. I've been seeded far away from home landscapes. I'm the progeny of those who deliberately smothered their cultural heritage. I epitomize a growing yearning for something intact, something with admirable longevity, something embedded in a specific place, something understood within the context of long-term, on-going lineage. I so want to be learned and trained in the ancient ways of my people. I want to recover and restore and remember. I want to hand down something full and rich to my daughter.

These things take time and support. In typical North American culture, we have a tendency toward recklessness and dabbling. If these kinds of things hold an interest for you, find a teacher and be cautious. I've learned to approach the Other World mostly through meditation, ritual, prayer, and art or craft. I've worked for many years with Mara Freeman of the Chalice Centre in Wales learning about Western Magic. I'm on my second year of learning with Dr. Daniel Foor through his courses and book on Ancestral Lineage Healing. I consider myself very much a novice.

For me, the revelations are still coming. Clues continue to appear. It's like a slow percolation of water into interstices. I pay more attention to emotional patterns now, to what I call tenderness tears. Those tears direct me. I'm fostering something. I'm cultivating relationships with the old ones, with my dead, my unknown ancestors, with the indigenousness of my Scots, Irish, English, and Bohemian people. I'm nurturing an identity incorporating my personal deep past. I'm aiming to assimilate the trials and the gifts of my lineage into my daily life. I'm in their debt. I seek their blessings and offer my gratitude. *They bore me. I carry them.*

2

The Landscape Road

One of the reasons I came to Erraid, to this tiny island in the Inner Hebrides, was to test a theory.

First, I must back up a way. There seem to me to be cosmic energies that pulse and fade like an invisible wave form, into, and out of, the collective consciousness. These energies manifest on our planet as intense curiosities or callings or desires for artistic expression and seem meant to bring forth certain kinds of knowledge or skills needed in the age.

Different people feel these energies across a wide spectrum—some just feeling an inkling, some becoming high profile teaching messengers for the rest of us. This happens around not only content or concept but also across time and space.

An idea comes to us we feel is original but when the research starts—there is that spectrum. One discovers a leading-edge cadre twenty or thirty years ahead of your own entry point. One gladly encounters people articulating with a magical clarity what one has been fumbling with for five years or ten years or maybe more.

So, I believe it is on planet Earth currently. Ancestral knowledge, old knowledge, indigenous mind, are all resonating, vibrating with vitality, and entering our awareness. A desire or call to reconnect with our people, our tribe, our ancestors is very much present in the collective field. Finding ways to follow the frayed thread back into a more authentic time are becoming primary. Startling awareness is building that our health and wellbeing being are inextricably linked to our relationships with our blood ancestors. For many of us this critical connection is broken, deliberately buried, misplaced, disregarded, or simply lost and forgotten.

Yet, we are called. We are utterly drawn to finding the way forward through the way back. The path leading away from distraction, compensation, avoidance, participation in a crazed consumer culture, and toward a deep past where our people were "indigenous" is compelling and seductive. We yearn for an ethos of place, continuity, and belonging. We long for a sane culture based on extended time in one place and profound knowledge of that places' abundances and limitations.

In answer to the longing, the desire, the call, many modern people are responding with various strategies. Some get at the work through traditional research of their lineage and with DNA testing. They are tracing the family tree. Some expand this work to ancestral healing practices, studying epigenentics, trying to break unhealthy family patterns or attempting to heal the trauma of ancestors who experienced something tragic and passed their trauma on.

Some access intergenerational information through the folk and soul music of their home cultures. They take a deep dive into the rhythms and songs and ballads of a people.

Some work on the larger patterns of diaspora and the effects of colonialism on their people. They may be laboring to preserve languages or reconstitute ceremonies or working to recover lost knowledge through dream work, ritual, and intuitive practice.

Every one of these strands interests me and I intend to learn more about them. However, the collective wave called me to the landscape road. I'm drawn to seeking access to ancestral memory through the landscapes that shaped my ancestors.

There is such a deep reciprocal bond between a people and their landscape. The "way-of-a-people" grows straight out of the resources of the land. The types of shelter, clothing, transport, ideal group size, seasonal movements, diet, and deities; they all emerge directly from the place. Landscape defines edges between known and unknown. The storied ground is full of names, legends, and shared history that constantly remind the people of the long continuity of relationship, of reciprocity. We grow out of a specific place on earth and that place is *deeply home*. The place of emergence. The mythic ground. The correct way and the taboo way emerge from place. The safety and the terror reside there together. The elemental discipline of landscape shapes the mind and the body and the psyche.

I wonder, as a daughter of diaspora, now generations removed from my place of origin, from my deep homeland, what can be learned from a deliberate, purposeful, intentional, return?

What might be felt, intuited, received? *What might I find on the landscape road?* What might be learned?

My objective on Erraid is now explained. Data collection is in progress. I explore the pink and grey granite, white sand beaches, islets and inlets, seals and limpets, mist, heather, and bog myrtle. I observe the flat grey water, the shimmering silver water, the turquoise and teal water.

I walk the boggy, squelchy, bracken covered hills. I listen for the lilt of the songbirds and scan for the silhouette of the raptor.

I'm gathering in, ground truthing my own anticipations, attending to expectation bias, all the while calling to my ancestors—calling to the ones that bore the ones that bore the ones that bore me.

3

Messages from the Neolithic

Across the landscapes of my ancestors (Scotland, England, Wales, and Ireland) there are ancient monuments. Stone circles and alignments, barrows and burial chambers, hill forts, henges, and quoits. These architectural wonders continue to astound and confound. Like a piece of art or music, the more you study them, the deeper the mystery around them grows.

Through the work of archeological researchers, we can glimpse the building of stone, wooden, and earthen monuments over thousands of years. They were constructed by people who were generally shifting from the hunter-gatherer Mesolithic into the Neolithic Revolution. Stylistically monuments seem to have stretched down coastal regions from the North, perhaps dispersed by seafaring peoples or by contact with the cultures of these people.

While some aspects of the Mesolithic hunter-gather cosmos appear to have remained intact—such as the concept of a tiered universe that could be accessed by shamanic techniques and profound connections to seasonal and multi-year natural cycles—other aspects of their cultures changed.

Burials shifted over time from communal to individual. The great wooden and stone circles and earthen henges were constructed, reshaped, and then changed again and again, reflecting on-going cultural changes in their structures, symbolism, and purposes. A stronger mirroring of the macrocosmic universe in the microcosmic landscape becomes even more important. The use of special stone, soils, careful positioning of monuments in the topography, and developing a deliberate wholeness in complex and extensive sacred landscapes grows. The sites appear to drift from social inclusion to exclusion at ritual sites.

Communal to individual. Inclusion to exclusivity. The great social changes of the Neolithic Revolution, resulting from the significant shift from nomadic hunter-gatherer ways to settled farming and skills specialization, were huge and are still reverberating.

We feel the implications of that immense change right up to the present. And not always in the most pleasant ways. In their scholarly book, *Inside the Neolithic Mind*, Lewis-Williams and Pearce, say, *"On the one hand, agriculture seems to Westerners to be a Good Idea, an advance toward civilization. On the other, it could be pointed out that domesticated plants and animals are more prone to catastrophic disease, and, in any event, farmers work harder and longer hours than hunter-gatherers. Perhaps this change was humankind's first Big Mistake."*

So, we find ourselves, 12,000 years on, wondering. Good idea or big mistake?

We are still much awed by a prehistoric world we apparently descended from; a world now shrouded in the hazy vapors of archaic time. By the evidence left, a rich, complex, intricate world indeed. It would seem to have been a much slower moving world even though it was changing radically. It was a symbolic world, where sun and wood and stone and stars and cycles of the moon held deep, long-term personal and cultural meanings.

It was a world of detected and manipulated subtle energies from the land, a place of connecting vibrations between earth and sky, a place of ley lines, blind springs, piezoelectricity, of magical acoustics and the songs or chants that made things appear and move in the chambers and stones. It was a spoken world, a world of memory, where thoughts and deeds and philosophies and religions were not recorded in our current way. It's a world that feels disorientingly foreign and hauntingly recognizable at the same time.

In our ever-expanding modernity, there are things we long for from that lost world and things that cause trepidation. We long for the incredible continuity, a multi-generational home landscape, the sense of shared vision and community. We long for a healthier, more abundant earth existing in a much less damaged state. We long for a world thinly populated. We long for enchantment.

We resist, however, the rigidity of a genuine tribal society; we shy away from the likelihood that the practice of sacrificing life (human or animal) in exchange for cosmic order was a part of social mores. We fear the rigors of an existence lived in harsh conditions full of back-breaking manual labor. Before it grew so unwieldy, before life became militarized towards the end of the Bronze Age, before the idea of kingdoms and underclasses, there was magic and toil, exquisite beauty in the symmetry of the cycles of the seasons, the dependable progressions of the heavens and, most likely, on-going deep apprehension about possible disruption.

Good idea or big mistake? What have we wrought in the last 12,000 years? Are there correctives? Restorations? Ways to reconnect to long ago patterns? The following are messages I received during my investigations of the Neolithic to Bronze Age at ancient monuments. They explore how to enhance our humanity, recover lost skills, and deepen our connection to the archaic whisper.

Message from the Neolithic #1: *Work to recapture your "mythic mind."* Develop the mythic mind, the storytelling mind, the playful, flexible mind. This is the mind that sees the fey, feels the dowsing rods clack together, knows the ancestors are not gone, seeks out the thin places, celebrates the rising of Venus, learns from the foxes and seals and spiders. Cultivating a mythic mind allows you to return to a much more animistic, multi-dimensional way of seeing the world. The mythic mind tolerates a fuller spectrum of reality. The mythic mind can decouple us from our constant linear thinking and allow slow time to return. It can help us rediscover the spirit of life that moves in all things. Reconnecting in this way allows us to glean information from subtle sources in the natural world: earth energies, animal and plant messengers, ancestral guides, and elemental spirits.

Message from the Neolithic #2: *Use gentle altered states to access information from your higher self.* Use altered states anyone can access, such as those afforded through dreaming, meditation, creating art, or light trance achieved with silence or through acoustic driving. Spending time in gentle altered states takes us beyond observations and interactions with the larger world and moves us into a much more interior space. These states allow for the entrance of corrective or developmental information to assist in our soul growth. A regular practice can help us identify our life's mission and purpose and help us to act on that information appropriately.

Message from the Neolithic #3: *Protect and preserve existing indigenous cultures and languages including your own.* Differing worldviews are critical as we move into the future. Too soon we lose the elegant inflections of variety and the richness and survival value encased in diversity. The delicate threads into the distant past are long indeed, but fragile, and existing indigenous cultures may have the strongest links to the more intact world we long for. Cultural extinction causes the same ripples in the great web as does the loss of a keystone species.

Aspire to re-establish links to individual lineages and cultures-of-the-past. We are all indigenous to somewhere—exotic weed though we may be where we landed. Through a study of your particular cultural background and history one can sense and value the range of human adaptation to landscape and cosmos. One can see our existence through a lens of ancestry, landscape, and culture-of-origin and understand ourselves in a deeper way.

Message from the Neolithic #4: *Wonder aloud about the efficacy and worth of our current cultural models.* Bravely examine the repercussions of the "Big Mistake." The Neolithic was a massive tipping point for humanity. We very well may be at another. Question the underlying assumptions in our systems, institutions, and economies. Think re-wilding, think restoration, think reciprocity, think collaboration. Question models of unbridled growth, of rampant individualism, of Darwinian competition, of ruling classes.

Good idea or big mistake? We find ourselves on that threshold again. Courage is required, my friends. It's a time of bravery in the face of chaos. We were born into it, our time, this place. Some say we are each here for a reason. Some say our times shape us. Some say we shape our times. Can we be stalwart, valiant, enduring, patient? Can we cross the threshold?

4

Ancient Monuments and Awe

Excerpts from a letter to B.W.

I'm looking forward to our conversations about awe, ancestors, death and other human mysteries. Recently, as I was visiting the earthworks here in Ohio, I got to thinking about how the impulse to monument-build is so strongly connected to creating awe in the visitors to the sites. It's still working too, after so much time and even within the context of a completely different culture. I was amazed and awed; and this from fragments and remnants. It's hard to imagine the impact "built spaces" like these must have had on people who had cultural references and deep meaning attached to the burial mounds, ditches, processional ways, and effigy mounds. Awe, I imagine, and reverence!

How we must need that awe as a species! To labor, over many generations it's speculated, with antler picks and baskets and copper tools to build a complex covering four square miles. And then to repeat these massive earthworks again and again in communities all along the river valleys. They are so reminiscent of the henges and earthworks in the UK that I was lucky enough to visit; though the UK sites are much, much older. Even though it is different in many ways, the visit to the Great Circle Earthworks at Newark, Ohio caused me to think of the impulse and effort that went into building downtown Chaco and the wide influences both cultures had across a vast landscape.

I can't stop thinking about that need to create awe. I guess it moves us to another state of consciousness, an altered view of reality, or maybe the "real" view. *Why is this so important?* It seems connected to our desire to link ourselves to the larger cosmos through monuments on the landscape. What a loss for us as modern humans to have mislaid that deep, deep connection to an ancestral landscape over generations in one place, filled with story and meaning. I'm not sure we can even grasp what might have been going on for them.

In my readings about the Avebury complex in England, I learned that when the great henge and stone avenues were built, the milky way would be seen as a circle in the sky as opposed to the arc we see now. The white chalk soils were exposed to make a great white circle on the land. It fills me with awe just to consider seeing such a sight; a thick circle of stars above with a white chalk circle mirroring that sky on earth. The Avebury people dug a ditch thirty feet deep with a flattened bottom; dug it with deer scapula and baskets. The tailings were used to create the tall mound around the ditch making it seem even deeper and grander. Seasonally the ditch filled with water as the ditch at the Great Circle Earthworks is also proposed to have done. Crossing water; magical barrier or protective ring? Traversing into another realm? Hmmmmm.

The processional way to Stonehenge is believed to start at the river and some archaeologists believe the monument was placed where it was to create the biggest impact on the viewer as they came upon it; it was not seen until it *loomed*. Downtown Chaco was also placed for visual impact. I expect most monuments are. Here in Ohio the earthworks were made to be open and unvegetated; to make an impact on people who were used to heavy forests and dense canopies with shaded light.

The Hopewell and Adena cultures oriented their monuments to lunar astronomical events more than solar ones. We see these same kinds of alignments to solar and lunar astronomical events in many ancient monuments. What keen observers and record keepers they must have been. Lunar standstills are about 19 years apart. I think of us moderns and our pathetic abilities to even know the current phase of the moon!

I think there are important things to glean from the ancient builders, but I am often stymied about how to access the information and to how make use of what I'm gathering. Deep time, the archaic whisper, that's what calls me somehow. These places of old power and awe, places where people followed ways that kept their world in harmony, that's what's been calling me.

Archaeologists find the most concrete evidence in funerary practices and make educated guesses about what was important or what had meaning related to death. I'm as, or more interested in what was happening to keep the opposite side of the wheel in balance. What was meaningful in work and life—what was funny? What was love like? How alike or different are we from them? As Paul Howe Shepard wondered, are the old ways recoverable?

5

The Magic of Cornish Monuments

Gorse is blooming bright yellow, sparse now, as we're well into October. Bits of purple heather stand above prickly leaves, tiny lilac-purple lanterns mixed with dry brown ones; what's left of their summer flowers. The wind is blowing cold off the sea. The sea is never far away here, hazing the distance with a blue slightly greyer than the sky. I'm up on the downs. Russet colored bracken ferns tilt at crazy angles, matted green grasses and clumps of reed grab at your feet, gorse and heather and berry-bramble roll along for miles. The skyline is broken now and then by granite outcroppings, the grey backbone of the moors. Lower down, toward the shore, are walled-in fields and stone houses. All around, everywhere, things are built of stone.

I'm up on the moor. High up and in a steady wind. This is where many of the old monuments are. Built in dramatic locations with a view. And of course, built of stone. Some of the cap stones on the quoits are estimated to weigh twelve tons. Impressive blocks of granite are placed upright in circles of "Merry Maidens" or laid flat in the ground to make burial cysts. Huge slabs are bridged over six-foot-tall stone walls to make a roofed underground tunnel called a fogou—one example I explored, sixty-six feet long. *Monumental* is the correct word.

I've been visiting sites in southern Cornwall for a couple of weeks. Mên-an-tol. The Nine Maidens. Lanyon Quoit. Carn Gluze. Carn Euny. Boscawen-ûn. Today I'm headed to Chûn Iron Age Castle, a hill fort high on the Chûn Downs and very close by, Chûn Quoit.

When I arrive at the hill fort, I move into the shelter of the stones, out of the wind. The big stones are piled three to four feet high and in a large circular formation. There's a standing stone just down slope of the entrance and in alignment, a bit further down, the quoit. I lean my back against a gritty giant and feel the heat of the sun. The stones are warm. They sparkle with crystals. They're covered in multi-colored rings and shaggy tags of lichen. As I settle in, looking back down slope toward the other stones, toward the sea, I think, they're still here, these massive stones. Coded messages for those who wonder, from the Neolithic and the Bronze Age, created 10,000 to 2,500 years ago. Still here. Still awe-inspiring. Still uttering something we can barely hear. Still arranged in patterns-that-speak on a living landscape by people long dead. *Are **they** still here?* The ones who made meaning from the stones, the seasons, the landscape they were embedded in; are they still here? Are they my distant ancestors? I sit quiet with the place, with the possibilities.

I wonder how they did the work; just the sheer physics of it. I wonder what the motivation was. I've moved some stones in my time, quite paltry in comparison, and it was not easy. These constructions, massive, complex, meaningful; required a tremendous amount of planning and labor. Required tremendous time and vision.

I wonder and marvel. I would like to float free in time, to see what they wore, the tools they used. I would like to hear their voices, understand a joke, know what was sacred. What differences would be apparent to them in having your bone and ash enclosed in a passage tomb, as opposed to a burial cyst? How long were ancestor's bones curated and why? What kept them building these awe-inspiring creations over such long periods of time?

The stones are silent. The wind insistent. I watch the ravens. I smell the crushed grasses under my feet. In the lee of the hill fort stones, there is a small patch of late-blooming heather. In the heather are brown butterflies with orange and white patches on their wings. I humbly ask the ancestors for a blessing as I leave.

Lineage Bearer: Sad Ohio

There's something close here, and constricting. Something sadder than it ought to be. Something that causes drag. It's memory maybe, maybe not even mine, that activates the now, like a latent virus moving along a nerve. There's something constantly unsettling, just short of reportable disturbance, perplexing and slippery.

There's something unhealed here, still festering. Something that smothers joy and distorts trust. There's something here that makes you want to go, to find another place, because you recognize there is no remedy. Only that drag. And no remedy. The disquieting sense of burden. Even the green and growing things can't overcome it. Not the songs of the birds or the bright colors of their feathers. Not the cleansing sun or the rain. No, the very ground is permeated with ugliness, it twines up the grapevines, falls with the leaves, composts into the soil.

I wake here disheartened, unmotivated, feeling like my dreams can't form, that the shape of things to come will be deformed and stunted. It's as if I'm caught in brown peat, waterlogged like a strangled bog creature.

Of course, there's a desire to shift the energy, to be the lineage bearer no more, to name the "something", to call it out of hiding for healing. But honesty is met with silence and kindnesses disregarded. The patterns are too strong, the dye set. There's a sense of leading horses to water and casting pearls before swine. You get tired. Weary. It's like water on stone, water wearing on stone.

Of course, there's appreciation for how we've all got here. Compassion for the slights endured. Understanding of the stinging arrows and the thousand cuts. Awareness of missing pieces, hidden pieces, the sharp wire, the snubs. Like bards of old, we could recite the litany of wrongs, list the misunderstandings, sing our versions of the sad shabby songs. Compassion doesn't equal approval. Because we can understand a circumstance, or a deep motivation, doesn't mean unpleasant behavior is sanctioned and accepted. Compassion doesn't mean dancing to the same old tune. Compassion doesn't give license.

Ancestors forgive me. I'm not the one for here, for now, for this. For me "it" remains unnamable, untamable. Hugely maddening. Maybe I'm faint-hearted. There's something unhealed here, still festering. Something that smothers joy and distorts trust. There's something here that makes you want to go, to find another place, other people, because you recognize there is no remedy.

My heart chooses exile. Withdrawal, tactical retreat, these strategies bring some variety of deliverance. Something like survival instincts take hold. Ancestors, progeny, please forgive me. Forgive me my faint heart, my lack of bone-deep persistence, my fading courage. I'm not the one for here, for now, for this.

Autumnal Equinox New Mexico

Scattered thoughts on landscape-ancestry,
landscape-love, time, and equilibrium.

September. In northern New Mexico a sweet yellow season sliding inexorably toward frost. Rabbit brush, chamisa, the dwindling sunflowers; all pure happy-making yellow. The squash vines are still reaching, terminating in yellow-orange trumpets and at night gingery-golden Jupiter is high in the sky. The thunderstorms are tapering off and the sky just above the yellow and cream rocks is a saturated electric blue, the perfect complement to lemon yellow and ochre.

We, coyote and I, rabbit and I, welcome the almost cold nights and sharper clearer air, snake is mumbling about his needs for mid-morning sun and how he's starting to think of where to sleep. It's a dangerous time for him between torpor and the continued hunt. The sun comes up later and sets sooner—the dark is stretching like a cat.

It makes me feel as if I'm floating, this time of year. Not exactly floating, adrift maybe. Caught up in a gentle circular gyre, an eddy, a stalled space in the middle of something. Living in some metaphorical Sargasso Sea. Becalmed between death and resurrection and highly aware of beauty, of transience, of how tenderly I'm balanced here on the edge of things.

We go 'round. Come 'round to this place of iterative balance. The place of equal light and dark. Of time suspended.

One moment I feel myself slip into the gloaming, into a deep past: the pink of a wild rose petal, seal eyes above steel grey water, a whiff of peat smoke, the taste of wild plums and hazelnuts, experiencing full sweet blackness and a relational sky. And then dawn, my symbol for the threshold into now, the present: the work of the day, paint brushes and silk, pink and blue tea pots, the feel of churro wool, the scratch of gone-to-seed tumble weeds on my bare ankles.

I'm living on some strange curving line, an imaginative mobius strip, looping back to stone circles and chalk, sea air and deciduous trees, then forward along the rust-red crumbly hills of the Chinle formation, smelling sage brush and spooking lizards from under junipers.

Back and forth, back and forth, from within a solid, durable imagining to current reality.

At once percussing quartz-rich outcrops near the Moine Mhor, pecking cup and ring into the rock, then smacking Rio Chama lightning stones together on a new moon night for a piezo-electric show. Black currents, then wolfberries. Ocean winds laden with mist, then desiccating western blows that suck the very juices from the stems. I love the dark. I love the light. I love the imagining and the now. I'm here and I'm there, present in the past somehow, bound in the long sticky strands of lineage and landscape-love. How long might my coracle spin in this salty eddy? I float on the lake in a plastic kayak, stop paddling, and am pushed by the incoming flow of the Chama, a slow swirl turning me around to the follow the current. Both. Then and now. The stark hills. The shifting light. Darkness. Light. Equal love. Equal appreciation.

Carefully balanced on the edge of these things, standing on the rim of the Rio Puerco canyon, I look over my shoulder to the west, in the direction of the dead. I find myself somewhere between celebration and atonement. Between tears of grief and heartache and tears that arise from receiving the swell of unconditional love that flows back along the twisting loop of the mobius strip.

Recognizing, at last, in part, the inherent reciprocity in past to present—present to past. There's pollen on the wind in both places. The magic of cross-fertilization is happening here and now in the half-this-half-that ephemeralness. I welcome it in its fullness.

Listen. Surf. Coyotes. Who were you born for?

8

Ways In: Finding Ancestral Leads

One: Tenderness Tears

Tear cairns. Like white shells lining a trail in the dark, tears are waymarks. These are not sad tears though, nor tears of joy, but a type that denote mysterious upwellings of tenderness. They seem to be about recognition, and deep memory, and are signposts that say, *pay attention, this is significant.* These tears, tenderness tears, mark for us lost soul-pieces, places of need, callings, and areas of necessary growth.

When I reflect, I see my life as a narrow winding footpath that's slowly resolving into a larger map. I look over my shoulder from the rise of a twenty-year-long slog and realize there have been many forks in the road marked by tenderness tears. Ah, in hindsight, I recognize tears were subtle clues. Clues about what's come, over that long haul, to feel like a predetermined destination. Tenderness tears reveal the "continent" and the "country" and the "town" calling my soul.

I finally see. I'm being *led somewhere.* I have found myself regularly seeking teachers, going on pilgrimages, and reading, reading, reading in pursuit of intense curiosities and odd fascinations. Passionate interests in subjects that seem to arise from nowhere clarify into signposts. But always, along the way, there were those hard-to-talk-through tears associated with the learning, with the desire. Tenderness tears. I understand them now as stepping-stones in a rushing brook or cairns leading over slick-rock, and I pay *way* more attention when they come.

It can seem peculiar how critical this tearing up is. Tears came while reading about relighting a perpetual flame in a goddess temple in Glastonbury; when hearing Angeles Arrien say that our ancestors look on us and think "maybe *this* will be the one to heal the lineage"; while sitting by a sacred well in Cornwall and ending up leaving a pound coin because I was suddenly in fear of the faeries; when being *called* to learn about ancestral family whose names and places and lives are complete unknowns.

Tenderness tears came often when I was studying and writing about the characteristics, skills, and ancient knowings that make and keep us human; while in training as a Sister of Avalon through the Chalice Centre; when joining in the Ancestor Roundhouse in Dartmoor, where women are caring for and listening to each other around the central fire; while pondering the incredible price of colonialism, of oppression, of diaspora, and how to heal the damage; when being called to craftmanship and using my hands to create beautiful and functional ritual items; when being blessed by and loved unconditionally by the ancestors. *The tears came strong and kindhearted when I felt, finally, my worth as one needed and important in the long line of my own lineage.*

The way in was tears. The upwelling of knowing that you are on the right path. These are the experiences that are drawn on the map over time, twenty years now, points along a pilgrimage, becoming a clearer and more defined road, a purposeful schooling by a sentient cosmos and well-intentioned ancestors and guides. On-the-job training through tenderness tears.

Two: Just Asking

I asked. I was given an image. There are women, a long line of them reaching back. They're each protecting a small flame. Their hands are cupped against wind, against societal forces that would extinguish the flame. There are many different faces, young and old, with red-orange light flickering across their features. They're steadfast in sheltering the flame.

I asked. I was given these images. They had to hide. Authenticity could mean a beating or worse for them. I toggle back and forth. There was coding and knowledge taken underground. I sense patterns in myself; indistinct resonances across time. I feel ancient bone-deep lessons expressing themselves in caution-atavism; epigenetic echoes of dangerous times. Developing strategies for safety, for stability, to avoid censure, to avoid being ostracized; I'm coming to understand these tactics as not only generally human, but as a personal ancestral burden. The wearing of a constant mask, concealing ones' true heart, continually editing speech; these were their methods, and these are mine. What's different is the degree and what's at stake. There's dilution but not resolution.

I was preparing to ask. I was learning to cast a circle of protection around myself in preparation for ritual. My mentor's instruction was to visualize a flame in my heart that would project out like an aura of shielding light. But there was no flame there. No blue light or white light or firelight. I couldn't conjure up a heart-flame. Why? I was deeply disturbed by this lack of light. I couldn't imagine a flame, but I *could* muster an ember. In my mind's eye I could see a small coal glowing reddish. A hidden flame? A flame as potential? I'm still not sure what this means, but over time my imagery has grown. I still don't see a flame at my heart. When I prepare for a ritual, I root deep into the Earth, clear to the molten core. I envision red-hot magma flowing back up along the root-hairs and rhizomes and into my heart. I see flowing lava in my core, red-orange glowing under black surface cracks; pahoehoe. The center of my chest becomes glimmering rocks in a sweat lodge, metal being annealed, radiant, pliant, an oblique light source, but not a flame.

The way in is asking. I'm trying to learn. I'm asking. I feel so unskilled as I attempt to communicate with my ancestors. I know we need each other and there is an important web of reciprocity to be re-established. Like any relationship attention is required, and listening, and tending.

I'm asking for healing of a lineage. I'm asking what they might like in the way of tending. I'm book-learning history. I'm researching the family tree. During this process, I'm given another image; beacon fires are being lit on hilltops one after another, extending back deeper and deeper into time. Huge flames. Flames that communicate.

It's the hour to step out; to stop suppressing who we are. We're a strong lot, this branch of the tree. Seafaring. Resilient. I'm a scion. It's the season for healing, for coming full circle, for seeing patterns and for reparation.

I'm asked to build a fire, to do so regularly, and to pour libations in the flames. Good whisky, high flames, wood to ashes, flesh to clay. Grandmothers, grandfathers, I sing your praises, in my gratitude, I sing you the bawdy songs you asked for. I build this fire in your honor. I let the sorrow and pain of your oppression break my own heart. I ask that your steadfastness and steel be channeled through my soul to strengthen me. I see your faces in the red-orange glow of the sputtering flame cupped in your hands. Bless your persistence. In your tender presence my heart flows magma, molten stone, metal and heat. I accept the sweet unconditional love you offer. I bring kindling to our needfires.

Three: Dreams and Imagination

I'm pulled back and back. Under the low black branches of yew there are rain-soaked needles half decayed. Are those footprints in the duff? There's disorienting fog, silver moony half-light, and the faint scent of blue peat smoke on a light and variable breeze. I'm feeling tension, almost anxiety, waiting to meet someone after years of absence and not being sure of my reception.

I'm spinning in the Otherworld, slow and expansive as a galaxy. Sporadically things appear and then wane; standing stones silhouetted against low grey clouds, the smoke-stained peeled poles holding up a thatched roof, a rocky narrow trail to the sea, dog-eyed seals bobbing in the surf, rusty bracken, frost-lace and thin ice on shallow puddles, hoodie-crows cawing, the smell of salt, iodine, and rot, the far-off rumble of waves breaking on pink granite older than human need.

Years pass. Years fly. Years crosshatch and fold. Fires burn. There are flames suffused with hidden meaning. People come and go like seasons, like moon phases, they bloom and fade, bloom and fade. We, this lineage, are as diffuse as argon in the atmosphere and at times as heavy as lead. I'm a bent twig on a branching tree. I'm the point of a spear. I feel the multitudes buried behind me and the restless possibilities before.

Time is crazy-looped and well knotted. Hand spun threads that might be flax, or wool, or maybe nettle, run through eras catching here and there on a basalt outcropping or the prickle of a thistle. Dream clues. Thin as a wood shaving and smelling of pine. Tentative as new love. Erratic as a rabbit on a runner. Illusive, shy, retiring clues. When I look head on all I see is wild rose petals rocking slowly to the ground and a glimmer of white. The glimmer; was that shifting sand, the fey, oily wool, ghosts, a tunic of linen? How will I know you? How will you find me? What is the esteemed question? The blessed answer?

Waking. Light trance. Sleep. The way in is imagining and catching dreams. It's as if I've always been awake; watching and waiting, gathering bits and pieces for some essential mosaic, some critical puzzle.

I imagine you on a crescent of white sand, sand dabs swimming over your feet, the blue sea stretching to the horizon. I dream of a squat home, blackened stone and smoke, fish and wool, wind and wind and wind. In my imagination you've handed me wild roses. Told me to study the seals and the stories of the seals.

It's as if I've always been asleep; numb to the call, drugged by the culture. I'm old now, and a such a child in this, so clumsy. I didn't know how. Teach me. Dream me home. Imagine me while I imagine you.

Four: Tending

I make a necklace from a scallop shell collected on a white sand beach in Scotland. I drill holes in the shell to hold a silver seal charm. I plant pink roses at my house. I follow the seasonal Celtic Wheel of the Year. I set a place for the ancestors at the table on Samhain. I build fires and pour whisky on the flames. I light candles. I travel to the landscapes my ancestors came from. I research the history of Cornwall in the 1400s and 1500s. I practice scales on a penny whistle. I work with wool, and hides, and sew linen. I try to learn Irish on Duolingo. I build a stone circle in my yard. I do ceremony. Honor the Crone. Sometimes in a litany I say their names.

I want to please the ancestors, feel more connected to my lineages. I'd like their help, their love, their wisdom. I believe they want to know me. I believe they are pleased that I've come calling. The way in, is tending the relationship. Small gifts, thoughtful remembrances, asking them and listening.

There are many ways in. Many ways. Simple ways. They are there, the ancestors, waiting, hoping even. Pay attention to what moves you. Dream, imagine, ask. Care for yourself and tend to them. They are there, waiting to help you.

9

Ancient Monuments and Special Stone

Stone was obviously an extraordinary substance to the Neolithic and Bronze Age monument builders. Certain types of stone were transported great distances to use in particular applications, such as the famous example of the bluestones at Stonehenge. The bluestones weigh in at between two and five tons each, and were transported approximately 180 miles, from the Preseli Hills in Wales to the plains of Wiltshire.

In their scholarly work, *Inside the Neolithic Mind*, David Lewis-Williams and David Pearce state their belief that people of that time saw stones as possessing symbolic/magical qualities. They believe for instance, that quartz was associated with death and transition and with water due to its shiny reflective properties. It was often placed at the entrances to passage tombs; a threshold space. Water and death/transition were also linked by symbolic crossings of water; by crossing real rivers and symbolically, the man-made henges did hold water seasonally or at the very least metaphorically.

Lewis-Williams and Pearce also speculate that the builders of stone circles probably viewed the stones as individual beings. Certainly, writers from Aubrey Burl to Paul Devereux, tell us about the faces, animals, or beings that people up to the present time perceive in the stones.

Others see the stones' characteristics as physically influencing energy flows and therefore the societal purposes of the monuments. Freddy Silva, author of *Legacy of the Gods*, says, "The ancients did not regard stone as some Victorian scientists once did, that it is nothing more than lifeless matter. To them, each stone held specific properties, because, quite rightly, every stone is made under different conditions. In the world of correspondences, the appropriate type of stone enhances the purpose for which the temple was created."

Silva goes on to say that certain stone was selected to anchor telluric currents at sacred sites. He says that stones with high contents of quartz and magnetite can be used to manipulate those currents. Michael Poynder points out in his book, *Lost Science of the Stone Age*, "Each stone carries its own chemical content. For instance, a granite pillar—used as a standing stone might also contain aluminum, quartz crystal, mica, and gold—all different elements that would influence magnetic polarities if the stone was used in construction . . . It is [a standing stone] likened to an acupuncture point in the landscape; a place we now know there will be an underground water and magnetic conjunction point; a natural power point."

In *Inside the Neolithic Mind*, Lewis-Williams and Pearce elaborate on their ideas about quartz and Neolithic perceptions. "First, we suggest that it may be a visual parallel between glistening, reflecting eyes and shiny crystals that often leads people to associate crystals with visionary experience. Sight and visions are both intimately associated with light. Secondly . . . when rubbed together, quartz rocks generate a bright, lightning-like flash of light known as triboluminescence. As long ago as 1880, Pierre and Jacques Curie discovered that certain crystals, including quartz, produce electrical voltage known as piezoelectricity."

Piezoelectric effects are caused by applying pressure to crystal formations, technology used in quartz watches and crystal radios. David Cowan, a dowser who has studied ley lines and standing stones in Scotland for many years, says that many stones in Neolithic settings show signs of being repeatedly struck. The ubiquitous "cup and ring" marks on stones in the U.K. and around the world being evidence of this repeated percussion. Hammering creates pressure within the stone which in turn creates piezoelectric effects.

"Hammering or percussing a rock or boulder—carving a cup-mark, for instance—causes the stone to emit a much enlarged 'telluric shadow' of that engraving."

One of the characteristics of chalk soils and the aquifers connected with them is that they too produce piezoelectric currents on a seasonal basis. When there is an abundance of water in the soils from rainfall it presses downward on the chalk subsoils. Piezoelectric currents are produced by that compression. A high percentage of crop circles form over aquifers in areas of chalk soil and along ley lines of telluric currents. There is a strong correlation of Neolithic monuments, crop glyphs, and subtle earth energies.

Another rather straight forward fact about chalk soils is their color. Ancient people exposed the white chalk as a startling contrast to the greens of the rest of the environment. Known as the "chalk effect," the surprising whiteness of the ditches and banks would have been, and still is, beautiful, significant, and noteworthy from a distance.

This information on the characteristics of stone, along with archaeoastronomy interpretations, and acoustic investigations at ancient monuments, leads us to surmise that the Neolithic and Bronze Age monument builders were working with a multi-layered, very complex set of social, scientific, and physical parameters as they designed and built these amazing structures. Their understandings and applications were not at all primitive. They may have been more sophisticated and subtle than we moderns by far.

10

Immense Continuity: Neanderthal Line

Homo neanderthalensis was living a successful life on earth for about 250,000 years. They had what archaeologists have tagged "immense cultural continuity." 250,000 years is *twenty-five times* as long as we have been agriculturalists and industrialists. Their bones and distinctive stone tools are found over an extensive range—from the British Isles to Uzbekistan. They lived in an incredibly challenging time climactically and survived the ebb and flow of ice ages in a cold harsh world.

The criticism most often leveled against them by modern humans eddies around their consistent lack of change over time. We scoff at their immense cultural continuity. Supposedly, that absence of change indicates a deficiency of intelligence. This argument is constructed based on evidence garnered about their material culture, almost strictly tool construction and use. Like the misconstrued word crone, popular culture uses "Neanderthal" as a pejorative. I disagree.

I have, like many people of European lineage, a small percentage of Neanderthal DNA. I'm delighted that this is true. I admit to a deep curiosity and on-going affinity for Neanderthals and celebrate the recent explosion of new research that brings more light to Neanderthal behaviors and intelligences. New techniques around ancient DNA collection and analysis, the re-working of museum collections and stratification data, as well as brand new archaeological discoveries have all brought surprises and additional controversy to the interpretation of the history of Neanderthals and Homo Sapiens.

I'd venture to say that the consensus now is they were not arm-dragging cavemen, but early hunter gatherers. They lived in small family groups, collaboratively hunted large game, ate a variety of plants, cared for the incapacitated over long periods of time, buried the dead, masterfully crafted useful stone tools, decorated and wore shells, perhaps made cave paintings, and most likely had some form of language, perhaps more in the form of song. One of the areas of hot debate is if they had a grasp of symbols. Their brains were at least as large as modern humans, sometimes larger. Maybe like dolphins, a large brain indicates a different type of perception, intelligence, and motivation. Maybe comparing Neanderthal intelligence with the thinking of modern humans is like comparing apples and oranges.

I like to imagine that long, long lineage. I like to imagine 250,000 years of existence without much social change—their immense continuity. I like to imagine 250,000 rounds of seasons, 250,000 cycles of dealing effectively with larger patterns—the oscillation of glacial ice, paying careful attention to the movements and habits of prey for success in the hunt, experiencing an animal-like connection to the present—perhaps experiencing deep contentment resting in the sun, pride in eking out a hard scrabble sustenance from the environment, of feeding a family through skill. I like to imagine the satisfaction of showing your child how to flake a perfect blade from a core of flint, of enjoying participatory singing. 250,000 years of practical survival. *Perhaps those things were enough.* Perhaps there was deep cultural satisfaction in on-going long-term rhythms and patterns. An immense contentment. That's a hard thing for a Homo Sapien to comprehend. It doesn't appear that the Neanderthal mind was obsessed with novelty, with change itself, as our restless minds seem to be.

In many ways they were genuinely like us. But *something* was different, something outside of, and foreign to, the kind of intelligence we currently value. Neanderthal life went on success-fully and expanded geographically for all those many years—and then an abrupt disappearance occurred after about 40,000 years ago. There is a passionate debate over what ended their long reign. The theories on their extinction range from a failure to adapt to climate change and other natural catastrophes like major volcanic eruptions, to war-like violence between modern humans and Neanderthals, to a lack of immunity to introduced pathogens and parasites, to competitive replacement, to low Neanderthal population densities and continued fragmentation of their populations as modern humans encroached on their territory. It was most likely a smorgasbord of deadly combinations that did them in. *We didn't outthink them as some used to claim.* The expansion of Homo Sapiens into Europe added burdens and pressures to an already stressed population and tipped a complicated run of Neanderthal bad luck over the edge.

We are fortunate that traces of their stories remain in their artifacts and their bones. I love to toy with speculation about them. To imagine them sheltering in their caves. To imagine the cold air drawn into their barrel chests. To imagine a group of tough, squat bodies, up to twenty percent stronger than a modern human, walking together on an icy path tracking red deer and aurochs, only sharpened wooden spears in hand. I like to dwell on their immense continuity.

Neanderthals are still within some of us, carried in our DNA. Sometimes I fancy my desire for an intact earth, a dark sky, and a longing for the chthonic—a respect for the wisdom that comes from the depths of the earth and the deities that dwell there—spring from a long, long line. Sometimes I imagine my desire for a walking-wandering "explore-for-food" life, carried out within a well-known landscape descends from a long, long line. From an immense continuity. Sometimes I wonder if my desire for a tribe, a working family unit, a singing-sharing group, derives from a long, long line. Maybe my inclination toward superstition, to believe in sympathetic magic, to practice light trance, was nascent in a sub-species from long, long ago.

I know this. And it's not imagination. I'm tired of noise. I'm tired of artificial light. I'm tired of rapid and repeated change. I'm tired of progress. Tired of novelty. I'm tired of growth, growth, growth.

250,000 years!

I imagine imitative singing with you way back then, clacking sticks or bones in a rhythm, bonding, unconsciously aware that I need you and the others for my very survival. In my mind's eye, I see a fire, kindled for gathering around and cooking over. We may be trance-dreaming of the Great Powers and finding ways to propitiate the Great Powers. In that vastness of unchanging time, I recognize, as you recognize, that we are in active reciprocity with the cosmos.

I fantasize my death along this immense continuity. I see the others excavate a natural pit in our cave. I'm tended by kin, placed in a fetal position, accompanied by flowers, then covered with a protective cairn of stones. At rest for 60,000 years. Excavated in 1960. My remains, my bones, my culture, the subject of intense on-going debate by Homo Sapiens. I wonder, are Homo Sapiens a flash in the pan? I wonder, where will the species be in 250,000 years?

Death

1

Arranged Marriage

Alladale: Fire and Shadow

in the brown heather
one adder wriggles.
over the arc of a stark crest
one black grouse bursts.

even entreated,
propitiated,
dream-maker doesn't come.

on the isle in the river
raven watches.
sleep is deep and black.

wind and water flow.
time flows.
each thing in its way.

my life escort, not dream-maker,
meets me.
we have been together a long time.

I used to ignore him.
used to begrudge this arranged marriage.
used to say hard things about him.
felt bitter awful things.

but I am softening.
my own bone and marrow.
skin, muscle, mind.

all these years
he has been faithful and I feckless.

when he comes each year
to circle me closer to the void,
toward the endless oneness,
when I take his skeletal arm
this time not resisting,
not twisting away
but shifting into wonder,
I see my mother's hand
resting on his forearm
just below his elbow.
at rest, relaxed, calm.

my mother's hand is my hand.
is the hand of the grandmother
I never met
and the hand of a nameless ancestor crone
who in her day
loved him more than
I *ever* had the sense to.

he has been ever faithful.
I feckless.

in this arranged marriage
as in some other lucky ones

affection is ripening
in the fullness of time.
I'm softening
and he is steadfast.

I'm coming to love this
boney being.

faithful, yes.
stalwart, constant as the north star.
constant as change, as mortality.

my hand is lying on his forearm,
at rest, relaxed, calm.
I turn my face as if to light,
turn to look up at that sweet skull,
see the curved line of a devoted
and trustworthy jawline
and feel myself smile.

2

I Long to be a Keening Woman:

A Ramble through Lamentation

Lamentation: the passionate expression of grief, mourning, sorrow, or regret: a song or poem that expresses sorrow for someone who has died or something that is gone.

Can Zoom provide a liminal space? Can communal ritual be successful online? Can we lament as a community through a screen? I guess so. I'm sitting at my computer, headset on, tears streaming down my face. I'm alone in my little wooden house, but with five hundred other people. Five hundred of us, all around the world, dropped into sacred space and offering prayer and ritual lamentation for those that have died so far from COVID-19.

Maybe online ritual isn't ideal, but it's something. A now sort of response. It's feeding a human hunger, a desire for companionship in times of woe. It's feeding a hunger for acknowledgement of shared misery, a hunger for structures within which we might process our grief. A public naming of what ails us. It's a place to gather, to take the time to place the proper importance on honoring the recent dead. A pandemic seems reason enough to call in the keening women.

There's great power in collective grieving, in making grieving public. We have an innate need, which has been systematically squelched, to make our pain visible and audible. We want to wail, fall to our knees, hack off our hair, smear our faces with wet ash. *But we don't.* We clasp our hands just so, turn away from each other and dab at our silent tears.

One must wonder at the invisibility of sorrowing in North American culture. We lack a tolerant, understanding community to hold us in our wild grief. We're taught to repress our deep mournful emotions. We seldom witness a person crying let alone wailing, weeping, or keening. Control is paramount. Being stoic the ideal. The average bereavement leave in the USA is three days. The societal undercurrent is to *just get over it.*

Mainstream western culture doesn't really believe the dead are still present or important to the living. Christian heritage is core to this suppression. Outward expressions of grief were thought to be pagan, heathen, and therefore unacceptable and were actively censored from the late 500's onward. Lamentation became an atrophied human skill. Does this loss impact the interpenetrated worlds of our recent dead, our ancestors, and us, the living? I believe that it does.

One of the most charming yet frightening books on this subject I've read is, *The Smell of Rain on Dust*, by M. Prechtel. In it he explains the relationship between communal and personal grieving, ancestor-hood, "ghosts," and problems of the living. According to Prechtel, examples of being well grieved include collective praising, lamentation, funeral fires, weeping, annual renewal of remembrance, actions taken to assure the person does well in the Other World, recitations of the person's personal and ancestral history, processions, food offerings, vigils, tending of the body, singing, and communicating to the ancestors that there is someone to soon be received. A list your local funeral director would be a bit aghast to implement.

Prechtel says that the energy generated by good grieving is the force that moves our dead loved one from this realm across a vast universal space to their initiation into ancestor-hood in the Other World.

The chilling part of Prechtel's work, the concept that I found so frightening, is that if our people are not well grieved, they literally can't make the crossing, and longing to stay in this world, come back to us as "ghosts." These ghostly souls will house themselves in the tenderest, most receptive members of a family. It's a terrible burden to carry an additional unmourned soul—the ghost "sucks people dry of their own future." These peoples' lives are sacrificed to the well being of the rest of the family. Symptoms that this has happened to someone include being fearful, nervous, and unsatisfied. The host becomes unable to complete plans, has split motivations—their loves, projects, and desires feel cursed and constantly unravel. They often have problems with mental illness, alcohol and drug addictions, and they become very hard to love. When that person dies, then there are *two* souls to push across, taking even more energy with a higher likelihood to fail, and it mushrooms from there. More and more unhealthy, hard-to-love ghosts are created. The community and culture have more and more troubles. *This construct makes an alarming sense to me and resonates with my lived experience.*

Instinctively, we hunger for a wild and free expression of grief, for the on-going creation of well ancestors to run interference for us in the Other World, to allow ourselves to feel *just how much we miss someone* lost to us—for more than the allotted three bereavement days.

We see these concepts echoed in Francis Weller's work, *The Wild Edge of Sorrow: Rituals of Renewal and the Sacred Work of Grief*. His "5th Gate of Grief" is called ancestral grief. One part of this grief is missing a relationship with the ancestors themselves, our Other World team. Another part consists of the burdens we carry of unresolved and unprocessed grief from generation to generation. This unmetabolized sorrow, like Prechtel's "ghosts," can also cause us trouble. Feeling numb, repressing anger, feeling depression, on-going sadness, episodes of addiction or eating disorders, magnified overreactions, chronic pain, and apathy are examples of the sorts of suffering that can surface. We can name it ghosts or epigenetics, the same dynamics are operating.

Our hunger for public grief and lamentation has also been apparent in the amazing success of Stephen Jenkinson's world tour called "*Nights of Grief and Mystery*," a couple of hours of lamentations and music on the human condition, death, lack of initiations for every age group in Western culture, disconnect from the ancestors, and our continuing abuses of the earth. Jenkinson's 2019 offering was received with packed theaters and sold out shows. Cultural hunger made visible.

My own hunger and need for public lamentation and public grief has been peaked this year. I went against my brother's wishes for no funeral or memorial because I felt a need to send him off with as much energy as we could so as to fill his sails to cross the void. I needed to offer a memorial, his friends and other family members needed to attend it, and I think my brother will forgive my transgression as he travels to the other world over the next year or so. I hope so anyway. And now COVID-19, and death showing up as deity, as a small "g" god, a force to be reckoned with daily and visibly, mortality's momentary vector a novel virus.

I'm as reserved and self-conscious as any other recovering-Catholic-turned-pagan. I mightily resist my tears, am totally inhibited when it comes to weeping and wailing and get paralyzing stage fright when I must lead a song. *And yet, and yet, I long to be a keening woman.* The bean chaointe, the keening woman of the Irish wake—once a respected, awe inspiring psychopomp, leading the community through her spontaneous vocal inspirations to the very edge of the grave and the very edge of this world—transporting the newly dead to the Other World on her praising lamentations.

What would that be like? Channeling that power? Letting the raw wild energies of the sea, the sky, the stones, *the life force itself*, flow through you—to be an instrument of that visceral potency—to traverse the thin places on behalf of your community, your people, your dead? *To know how, to be willing?*

I ask you again, what would that be like?

3

Loss in Avalon:
A Pilgrimage Story

Each morning for three days running I've climbed the Glastonbury Tor. I go up the steep back way on the path less used, through the apple orchards, laden now with stripy red apples. As I climb, I think about the legends of old Avalon. About the magic and the mists. About the women and the apples. The "now" apples are fragrant, ripe, and dropping. I pick up a windfall to eat. I wipe away the dirt and bite around the bruises. Women and apples. Dirt and bruises.

At the top, I sit and look out over the Vale of Avalon, now bronze-gold fields stretching away as far as the eye can see. The patchy clouds cause the sun to slant through in silvery fans of light. They are like "god rays", the light you might see in a religious painting. I sit in cool breezes while leaning against the Christian tower built over a pagan site. From far away, the tower I lean on looks like a nipple on the rising breast of the Tor.

As the breeze blows and the light wavers, I imagine the Vale as it was long ago, not an agricultural valley but a shallow marshy sea. I imagine shifting mists and leaning reeds and waterfowl lifting up in those fans of light. I imagine women poling wallowing boats, intent, on their quiet way to the island of the apple trees, to Avalon, the Tor.

Unusual thoughts have sidled up near me here. Women's notions I guess, emotional recollections, long forgotten fluxes of memory. I find myself conjuring up things that didn't happen but might have. My sisters have materialized fog-like, my mother and her mother too, solidified ghosts, greeting me from the condensing mists hanging over a shallow sea that no longer exists.

What if my sisters had lived? One older than me that shares my name, one younger named Miriam. How lovely it might be to have them in my life now as I age. I would have a different name; I might be Miriam and then what name would Miriam carry? The name Miriam means "wished-for-child" or "sea of sorrows." Did my mother know that, choose that name in her loss?

Maybe we would have traveled together like the sisters I've seen on this months-long pilgrimage; maybe we'd be walking up the trail of the Tor together. Laughing together, faces different and yet the same. They would be company and companions and family. How unexpected, unforeseen, to think of them here, now, on the slopes of the Tor. I'm suddenly sad and sorry they didn't get a chance at life. I suddenly miss them.

What if my mother, Marian, had been healthy and strong? What if I was holding her elderly elbow today, her long grey braid swaying down her back as we explored some ancient site together, had tea and scones and chatted. She is twenty-six years dead; me, forty-eight years absent from the place where she raised me. No companionable walks, no mother-soul-shelter in an emotional storm.

What if her mother hadn't been a raging alcoholic, so sick and sad and uncomfortable in her own skin? What if my four-year-old memories of my grandmother, Anastasia, were about playing together, or cooking, or hearing a family story again and again instead of remembering scary silence. All I can recall is watching her die from cirrhosis of the liver, her small body curled up in a fetal position on her couch. She was covered with a colorful patchwork quilt. I watched, timid and worried, as my mother tended to her, I, having been sat on the porch to be out of the way. There were iridescent green hummingbirds zipping around in the orange trumpet vines as I gazed at mother and daughter through the screen door.

In this place of apples, of women, of dirt and bruises, I feel my forlorn females like a fresh fall on gravel, knees and palms stinging and scraped. I tenderly finger the size and shape of what we missed. I feel disappointment like a wasp sting. I suffer a generational gap, like a lost tooth, and I can't help putting my tongue in the empty socket and tasting blood.

At the base of the Tor there are two wells, two springs, one white and one red. I go to the Chalice Well, the red one. Go to the healing female waters. The red water is icy cold, but I take off my boots and socks, roll up my pant legs, take off my coat and pull up my sleeves. I soak my feet and lower legs in the rusty pool. I fold at the waist and lave my hands and arms and face. I drink from the red spring. Drink again. I feel instead of think. I sit in long silence at the well head, the holy red well, and let tears roll down my face. Tears for my sisters who never had the chance to cry, tears for my mother who never felt welcome, tears for my grandmother, in so much anguish she slowly killed herself. Tears for me too, larval crone that I am, serving as a more and more willing conduit for the unhealed, unresolved suffering of my lineage. *I resent this crippled world that made me forego their gifts.* I console myself; I reassure my "we-don't-cry-in-public" core that this release isn't silly or self-indulgent or sentimental or maudlin. It's grief. Simple and true. Grief.

In this place of women and apples, high up on the Tor again, I envision the Vale filled with water. Covered in breathing mists. The vaporous water is a holy barrier hung against normal time—linear time—a living curtain hung against what we believe is reality. There are gentle zephyrs stirring the haze. Tall reeds are nodding and tapping in the tender ripples. There are slanting fans of silver light piercing the veil like auroras.

Those women I miss? The babies we never knew, the mysterious mother and grandmother? I see them emerge from the vapor. Like lost love found, they swell like pink rose buds. Then become birds. Beating with flight, they rise off the water; herons, swans, geese. Their beautiful wide wings spread like goddess light. They are slanting rays of silver.

4

Maybe How Death Is

You know how things can look so different in different light or in fog? I walk the same trail daily. I drive the same road into town more often than I'd like. But sometimes I'll suddenly feel off track. *Where am I? Where am I exactly?*

The well-known in strange misty light, or evening-not-morning light, or in storm light, can suddenly be odd, peculiar. The shadows aren't right. The curve ahead seems like some other curve. It's not terror you feel, nor panic, but something like it, diluted down. It's akin to self-doubt maybe, or like the universe is gas-lighting you. It startles you into looking around, looking up, finding a more distant landmark to anchor you.

This shifted reality happened to me out on the trail not long ago and put me in mind of my older brothers, who were forever trying to terrify me. One of the things that worked best for them and would give me that naturopathic dose of panic was a distortion of normalcy. They would pull a nylon stocking over their faces (remember real nylon stockings?!) and it would stretch and flatten their faces. They still looked familiar as they jumped from behind a door—brother-but-not-brother—and that was *so much worse* than a witchy Halloween mask. Your perception of reality bends, a skewing of the known into a curve that seems like some other curve.

Some other curve. I remembered an incident that gave me that same rise of fear. It was such a benign setting, such a normal thing. I came home late from a meeting on a moonless dark night with lots of stars. I was in the car I'd been driving for at least five years. When I parked the car and reached for the door handle, I just couldn't find it. That automatic motion brought me up short. *Where am I?* Whose car is this? I literally had to feel all around the interior of the car door for the handle. My disoriented brain was shouting; the light is different, the shadows aren't right, this is some other curve. How did that reality misfire happen? That handle should've been right where I'd reached a thousand times before. But it wasn't.

Sometimes I think dying might be like that. A sudden, or maybe not so sudden, distortion of "normal" reality. A body, a place, a spirit, that's become oddly different, not where you'd reached a thousand times before.

In the cultural tradition I have the most faith in, it's believed that a person who's died will linger near their earthly body for about three days. I wonder about that transitional time, the time of the misty curve, the time of the different light, as a time of looking around, looking up, finding some new distant landmark with which to anchor ourselves.

People were tended to during that in-between period with vigil. In my "now-I'm-dead-and-here-are-my-last-would-be-instructions" envelope, I've asked my daughter and my friends to do this for me; to sit with my body for a few days while I get my bearings. Get the dry ice, kiddos, and play me some tunes, I've left a song list.

And for heaven's sake, no burial. I'm far too claustrophobic for that. No, my hope is for a hot, hot fire—preferably a real one, a cord of juniper and pinion pine—to act as a catalyst. To send me, the visible part, now I've oriented to where I am, off on a final phase-change. To transition, at least for now, to vapor and ash.

If my daughter or friends want to, I invite them to sift through the ash for the bone bits and melted gold teeth blobs. To use those intimate and enduring pieces for rattle sounders or to store in a pretty box for setting on the ancestor altar at Samhain next to the whisky, or to take me along in a pocket to special occasions. I'll do my best to be there when needed. The rest, the fine ash, I'd like to dust the places I love. To rest my tired old molecules on what sustained me during one life, one mysterious round. Sun-warmed red-rock, certain small Hebridean islands, high wind-swept granite outcroppings on the moors, wild undammed rivers, and the cold upwelling sea.

I don't believe that death and the afterlife are all that sweet and pure. I imagine all we do is keep on learning. But I hold out hope for a bit of rest, for a breather.

I hope that when I reach for something, it's there. That the different light is improbably beautiful, that the shadows are purple-blue and somehow familiar. I hope that around the curve, some other curve, in the misty reaches, will be my old ones come to gather me in. I hope that they will be paddling coracles or riding fat-bellied horses, necks arched like swans. I hope that in the moment of meeting they will wrap me in warm woolen blankets near a beach fire. I hope I will settle comfortably into long deep belonging.

My Brother's Death

winter 2020

Ashes. Mixed all through the knee-deep squalor—cigarette ashes—grey and dusty and reeking.

I arrived in Ohio late Christmas night, so saw his house twelve hours before I saw him in the hospital. When I stepped into his kitchen the severity of the situation was clear. All through his place, all over the floor and every surface, there were dirty clothes, empty water bottles, dishes and pots and pans filled with molding food, ginger ale cans, over-the-counter remedies, shredded cat food bags, empty cigarette packs, small green propane canisters, bloody bedding, and five gallon buckets of excrement. A frightening chaotic jumble of disorder littered everything.

I hate the smell of cigarettes. *Everywhere, ashes. Cigarette butts.* He was a life-long chain smoker.

This is not my brother Dave's style, dirty chaos. Not at all. When I saw the mess, I knew. This is *bad*. Really, really, bad.

It took me a week to get from New Mexico to Ohio after coordinating a 911 call with his neighbor. Calling 911 in New Mexico doesn't get you emergency services in Ohio. Helping from a distance—trying to judge how much he was hiding—was problematic. He was trying to tough it out, to not be a bother. *Damn it.*

I knew he was *really* sick and *really* scared when he called in mid-December to say he thought he was dying. He lives alone down a long crappy road. He admitted he had no heat, couldn't make it up stairs to the bathroom, and was not willing to ask friends for help. *Shit. Shit. Shit.* I'm so far away. *Days away.*

For a day after his phone call, the lines were lit up. There were calls to Ohio county services, calls to my daughter, calls to my other brother whom I seldom call. Advice and conferring, information gathering, crying, and finally deciding, against my ill brother's wishes, to call to

911 through his neighbor in Ohio. Even though he didn't want to go, at least now I could rest, and hopefully so could he. He was in a hospital, somewhere clean, with heat and food, and professional people to try to untangle what was going on.

It didn't take long for the doctors to diagnose small cell lung cancer as the main event with a constellation of other lesser maladies on the list. Words like terminal, aggressive, palliative radiation, chemo, showed up on our horizon like a row of henchmen.

It's become a blur of days. Getting to Ohio. Cleaning the house. Driving back and forth to the hospital. Trying to understand what we were dealing with. Decoding medical talk. Trying to get a clear picture of options. Learning the lingo of a terminal diagnosis and oncology people. Talking about death without talking about death. Watching my brother process *two to six weeks*. Two to six weeks without treatment, maybe several months with.

Dave had always mistrusted the system. He'd waited *way too long*. By the time he got to the hospital he was already so frail, so thin, so eaten by the disease, he was a skeleton. He was so weak he couldn't walk out of his hospital room. The doctors said there was no time to allow him to build up some strength. Aggressive. Terminal. They told him he might buy time with radiation and chemo. At this point in the story, I was still in New Mexico, still hadn't seen his condition in person.

He asks me over and over, what should he do? What would I do?

You can't choose for another no matter how much they want you to. How could you ever know what you'd do in their shoes—what you'd choose—given two to six weeks? When push comes to shove, holding on has immense power. Going on living a monstrous pull. The cancer doctors encourage the fight, use war metaphors, intrinsically foster a feeling that it's wrong to "give up." They pummel us quietly with a never-say-die leitmotif. Dave surprised me, surprised himself I think, and chose to try treatment.

After beginning one round of radiation and chemo, started before I arrived from New Mexico, and taking about two weeks, he called me late at night from the hospital in a panic. I was back on the farm by then. He felt even more awful, sicker, more anxiety ridden. He thought his death was imminent, that night, and he wanted me there. The hospital was an hour and a half away. We talked and I reminded him that what he was feeling was most likely the symptoms of the treatment showing up. He calmed down. I tried to. I drove to the hospital in the morning. He was stirred up again and asked me several times, "why would anyone choose this?" What could I say? Life keeps calling, I guess. We are not familiar with death; we artfully avoid it. In our culture we fear we just disappear, feel there will be no long-term remembrance. We harbor no surety that our old ones are gently waiting to guide us on the other side. It's disturbing, this dying process, it feels dangerous and terrifying; that's why people choose treatment, choose this.

After finally learning what I needed to ask for on his behalf, we had a meeting with the palliative team, the comfort and quality-of-living folks, and got on the hospice floor as opposed to the oncology one. Dave's goal at that point was to *get home* and die on the farm. It took quite a few more days and was touch and go as to whether he could be cared for at home. He was frustrated and restless. I was afraid of not being capable.

Luckily, whatever powers for good there are in this cosmos sent my older brother Ray and his wife Marlene, and my daughter Maya, into this demanding process with me and Dave. Death seems to reveal our true networks. We look over and find out who is beside us in the trenches, throwing a shoulder to the gritty, repellent, inconvenient, time-consuming tasks involved in dying.

Dave knew he wanted to die at home. I made him a promise that I'd be there when the time came, and I did my best to fulfill that promise. He had no family other than siblings. We got him home to the farm and his cat and the wild birds twenty-two days after his original 911 ride to the hospital. He hung on at home for another month, mystifying the wonderfully gentle and competent hospice nurses with his perplexing and extraordinary tenacity.

Health and sickness seem to operate with an element of fate, of fickleness—yet you can see some things coming and probably shouldn't be surprised. Dave chain-smoked since he was a teen.

It's a years-long sad tale, like so many in our world today, replete with strands of long-term family dysfunction, a powerful American sense that we can take care of ourselves goddammit, and a total lack of any real community. We're each alone with our looms, weaving sad threads into a tight cloth. It's a cloth full of slubs and imperfections. When life subjects us to a three-cornered tear we fall right through. If we're lucky, someone comes along to pick us up, even if we think we don't want them to.

If I've learned anything through this experience, it's that dying is crone's work. Wisdom's work. There are big doses of grim tough things to swallow as well as the occasional sweet delight.

Tending death triggers such a dance of feelings: love, resentment, sorrow, disappointment, gratitude. It also throws you ice-cold and ill-equipped into a churning sea of memories, anxieties, doubts, confusions, uncomfortable decision making, and just plain exhaustion.

Stephen Jenkinson says death is a god or diety one *must* accommodate, and I think that's true. It's unpredictable, surprising, and alarming, though it happens to all of us. It's a force of nature like a tornado or a flood or a landslide; we are carried along on its energies and they are much grander than we are. We are humbled by it. Unsettled by it. Reminded by it.

Life/Death/Life. Life/Death/Life. We are all shaped by the tough tenderness of living, loving, and dying. Heart-wisdom comes out of crone work, seeds grow out of the dark cycle.

The broken open places in your soul, the enigmatic complexity of death, these are the cracks the seeds fall into. The roots take hold, the stone erodes, the cotyledon unfolds. There is Love in all of it.

6

Visitation at Petroglyph Point

In Memory of Marian Jean (Cornish) Cross
1923-1994

in this place of memory
where the rock once knew water
stretching off away to a long-ago horizon
and the hands of men carved temporary meaning
into the flanks of the stone,
my mother remembered me
from her place on the other side.

she looked down at me
from her heart-shaped face
as she flew above me
on silent buff and white wings
and let loose a feather
soft with reconciliation.

I traced its slow fall
over a field littered
with a million tiny bones.
mouse and rabbit.
the small white jaws and ribs mixed with the reddish sand and grit
on a lakebed long missing its water.

I found the feather lying on a place
where the sheets of time overlap.
the wind there makes the softest whistling sound
as it fingers the slowly eroding grooves of the petroglyphs.

7

Between Earth Day and Beltane 2020

Since I came home from Ohio and tending my brother Dave's death, I've been sleeping hard and deep. Occupying dreamless space. Just gone somewhere. I'm not waking until Jupiter is leading Saturn and Mars across the pre-dawn sky. I've been watching them for a while now, bunched up then stretched out, three bright planets—recently meeting up for a few days with the waning moon. They're striking but for some reason slightly disturbing—as if they're trying to convey some malign portent or omen that in my drowse, I can't quite grasp the meaning of.

That's my start most mornings this spring (outside world in turmoil or not) quietly staring at those planets staring down at me. I wrestle with my pillow to keep Jupiter in view, tug the quilts up over cold shoulders, adjust my sore hip, snuggle closer into the cat curled behind my knees and watch the light come up, pink and silver-blue. Dwelling in some liminal place in that dawn-thin time, I slip back and forth between sleep and awareness. I'm physically uncomfortable and restless. I feel the weight and press of the times maybe, or sense a call to unashamed lamentation, or know bone-deep the disappointment of just how unprepared I am—how untrained—how unskilled.

The things I need, we need, our culture needs, have been lingeringly ignored or cruelly suppressed or carefully hidden for so long there's barely an echo. I'm old now, (nearly *two* lifetimes of my Neolithic forebearers) my opportunities for schooling in these things limited by my culturally triggered ignorance and inexperience, my time seemingly too short in human form for ever learning the intricate critical things necessary for a true and trustworthy life—too short even to identify exactly what those intricate critical things are. In the silver-grey light of daybreak, I feel a sort of keening soul-regret, a suspicion I've been inadvertently betrayed by my people. I feel demoralized and disheartened by my culture, suffering an on-going, grief-inducing, irreparable loss at an ancestral, cellular, anthropological level. Maybe that is the sad message in the planets I half perceive, why they disturb me in their cold elemental beauty.

None the less the days move on—come and go. I walk in the harsh desiccating spring winds. Find bear tracks in the dust and smell juniper. Do studio work or gardening. Prepare food. Brew tea. Think and study. By three or four I fall asleep again, hard and deep. Afternoon comes and I'm away with the faeries occupying more dreamless space. For a few hours, I go someplace nameless, unmapped, dark, and enduring. I'm just gone. Absent. It's strange, spending so much time with this blank, bottomless visitor, sleep. A visitor that used to be illusive. And who is, oddly, at the present, bestowing on me hours and hours of black, empty company. Welcome company, I think, but still peculiar, an uneasy stopover, like a friend you haven't seen in years appearing on your stoop—and though remembered, the renewal of acquaintance feels slow and awkward.

I wonder sometimes where I'm going during those vacant hours. And what I'm doing. Possibly, I'm learning something on the slant that I can't understand or make conscious. Or maybe I'm just exceptionally, profoundly tired. Doing absolutely nothing. Nothing at all. No story. No meaning.

Speaking of strange, odd, malign, tiring, and profoundly peculiar, 2020 continues its haring path of uncertainty and drama. I've been following the news cycle more than normal (more than is good for me I'm sure) because I can't help being perversely fascinated by the global sociopolitical story—it's so much like a mix-up of a daytime soap, Saturday Night Live skits, and noir fiction. Theater of the Absurd writ large. *Whew—no wonder the sandman is after me.*

One of the virus juxtapositions that left me tender and wondering is the wide gap between how old people are perceived by the Navajo and Pueblo peoples here abouts and Western cultures in general. I've heard such venom in #boomerremover, the far Right's willingness to sacrifice life for "economic stability," (whatever the fuck that is) implying that it's just a lot of old people, people of color, and low income folks dying anyhow. I see the Marie Antoinette-like, "let them eat cake" entitlement of the rich—going to small, remote places to hide out and play while potentially bringing the virus to under-resourced areas of the world.

The Navajo and Pueblo people are deeply concerned about losing their elders—their wisdoms and love and presence. It's so different—living in extended family multi-generational households, perhaps not having access to running water, often being in more remote places without medical services. So different.

I've come to deeply resent the American whining about not being able to go to hair salons (my roots are showing!) and enjoy meals out—*what terrible sacrifices people are making!!* It's ludicrous and embarrassing, as so much is about modern culture.

All we can do is make the best of this kind-of-half-good-half-bad pause in "normal" life. It does beg reflection, no?

There's been some shrewd, thought provoking things said by people I respect. It's hard to predict what will happen next, but my expectations are low. There'll be more perils to come with greater frequency I imagine, and it might be time to learn to hunker down, pace ourselves, and try to marinade in all those daily small wonders. Sometimes I think all this is just making what's always there more visible; uncertainty, our illusion of "progress," our undeniable inter-connectedness with the ecology of the planet, our uneasy relationship with death, our unending desire for meaning.

Here's hoping we humans find a new way through the hills ahead. Build up our psychic fires so we might find each other in the dreamtime.

8

The Story from Afar

In Memory of Raymond Clifford Cross
1926-2008

The slow curl.
The reverse of unfolding.
The drawing in.

They tell me the story.
I'm far away.

For me the awareness comes and goes.
The years are untethered,
time unhitched.
There is the black and white pony,
the long rides for coal.
We are fishing for blue gill,
then bringing in the hay.
There is a thunderstorm brewing.
I hear him down there in the winter dark
loading the stove.

We speak over wires and thousands of miles.
Small mundanities, small talk,
as if this is any other day.

How is your child?
How is your husband?

I say I wish I could be there.
He says it is too far to come.

They tell me the story.
I'm far away.
He fades and dapples like afternoon light.
They tell me the story.
They wait and watch.
The hospice comes and goes.
The nurse tells them what to expect.

The slow curl.
The reverse of unfolding.
The drawing in
to a fetal position.

And when they are all outside,
and he is finally alone,
he takes flight from the tightening bud.
Leaves behind the in-folding flower his body has become.

9

The Hardest Thing

The hardest thing is how the mind holds on to certain images. The dog getting hit by a car, the friend collapsing, the beetle killed forest, the house fire. I'm seeing, over and over in my minds eye, my brother's last week.

He was incredibly thin, very much a skeleton. His skin had turned leathery and oddly stretched over his bones like a living mummy. All his hair had fallen out due to the one session of chemo he tried, and his face was sunken and skull-like. His eyes however, stayed the same until very, very, near the end.

He and I looked alike. We shared coloring, curly hair, and hazel eyes. Sometimes, when I looked in his eyes, I felt I was looking at my own end. His eyes were alternately teary, afraid, full of courage, and surprisingly, until he became unresponsive, full of humor.

As the days of hospice wore on, I had a harder and harder time looking at him and touching him. This reluctance made me feel weak and disappointed in myself. I had to clean out his mouth with sponges, his mouth was full of thrush, and near the end I could barely stomach it. He looked so like a classic movie monster. Yet I knew in my heart he was just my older brother Dave, the kind one, who had always been my safety net. He needed gentle kindness, not revulsion.

Aversion was a presence though, as present as the family ties: duty, kept promises, and love. I hope he didn't sense that revulsion I was feeling. I tried not to let it show or let it stop me. I was ashamed of my inability to overcome that sensation.

The horror of those image-memories rise up when I'm trying to sleep. My mind's eye mercilessly plays the movie of those last days repeatedly. I'd rather my mind would remember him tan and laughing, healthy flesh on his bones, growing vegetables and flowers.

These memories aren't linked to regret, or guilt, but to sorrow. They are tied up with dismay about the way he died, the sadness inherent in his life choices. I feel settled, firm in my sense that everyone involved did their best, including myself.

Maybe, as with other shocks, like accidents or relationship rifts, the ugliness will fade in time. Soften. Shift. Become indistinct. Maybe, over time, the kinder things, the praise memories, the healthier happier face and smile, will grow in proportion, gain depth and color, be the kept files.

10

The Story of Sam

Sam came into my life at a difficult time. My marriage was ending as well as my stable life in Tucson. My soon-to-be-ex-husband was north in Oregon, and my daughter, Maya and I were living in the family house down south. Both of our cats had died of old age in recent years and Maya and I were very much missing having a cat. My husband was against getting a new cat for several reasons, most of them, I must admit, practical. But Maya and I were really, really wanting a cat. And my husband was really, really saying no. He was away for a few months. So, feeling free and rebellious, released from my husband's influences, one impulsive day, we went looking for a cat.

It was an all-day exhausting adventure going from rescue places to public animal shelters. We'd just about given up. At the last minute we decided to stop at an adoption event sponsored at a pet store. There was Sam. A mellow looking stripped cat with a brownish nose. He was a big fellow and didn't make Maya sneeze; one of our primary tests of compatibility. We liked him immediately but with an abundance of caution (ha ha) went to have a late lunch and ponder the wisdom of bringing a cat home at this juncture in time.

Of course, we talked ourselves into Sam.

Sam had only been in the shelter system for a few days. His owner had died and left Sam without a home, a relatively common occurrence in a retirement community. He was quite beautiful, part Abyssinian, part something that made him wildly tabby colored and HUGE. Sam weighed in at twenty pounds but wasn't in the least fat. Sam went home with us that afternoon.

This was just a few months before absolutely everything in my life changed. My husband came back to Tucson. Things were strained to say the least. He was not happy about a cat in the house and Sam didn't help matters by poking minute claw marks in my husband's new leather couch. It was a stand-off in many ways. We discovered then that Sam preferred men and constantly made lovey overtures to my resistant (at least in my presence) husband.

March, April, May. We all survived, I guess, and went our separate ways. My husband back to Oregon, now my official ex. My daughter went to live with her boyfriend also north, and Sam and I took to the road like gypsies. Sam and I headed first for a stint in Ohio, back to the farm where I grew up and where my older brother Dave still lived. It'd been over twenty years.

Sam took to farm life, never once mentioning his old urban existence. He loved the freedom—the farmhouse was a good mile from any roads—he loved hunting, spending many an hour staring stock-still into the grasses in the upper field. Sam also took to my brother, which was wonderful, as Dave was lonely and had lost his dog a few years before. Can you see the direction this is going?

Before arriving, I'd let Dave know my plans for an extended stay in Scotland and England and asked if he'd be willing to take care of Sam. He was happy to have Sam's company and mine for the time I planned to perch in Ohio. I kind of knew that Sam would shift his allegiance to Dave, and that Sam wouldn't really be interested in traveling with me all over the world as I intended.

Sam became Dave's cat rapidly and readily. People who know my brother, who knew my brother, told me later that Sam truly enriched my brother's life. They speculated, and I believe this too, that Sam might've even extended my brother's life. Sam became quite central to Dave, who was quite ill, but wouldn't acknowledge his illness.

Dave and Sam were together there on the farm for about five years. When I phoned to check in on Dave during my travels and after I'd moved to New Mexico, there was always a good Sam story or two. Sam joyously chasing the falling leaves. Sam jumping onto my brother's belly from the top of the dresser at four a.m. wanting his breakfast. Sam, the king of the pillows. They were good company to each other.

This past winter the cancer that was growing in my brother's body finally became inescapable and undeniable. He was near death, but we weren't positive about it. He was in Ohio still on the farm, and I in New Mexico. There was a difficult messy time, with me on my way, and Dave in the hospital. Dave was worried about Sam. A neighbor was giving him food and I was working on getting there.

Sam was very happy to have a human in the house, cleaning up the place, and getting a nice warm fire going in the furnace. I wasn't Dave, but I'd do.

While my brother was in the hospital for about three weeks, I'd bring him phone photos of Sam in his basket by the heat register, or eating from his bowl, or just watching birds out the window. It was a reassurance that Sam was doing OK. However, my brother wasn't.

Dave wanted to die at home, and we managed to get him down to the farmhouse, ensconced in the same kitchen room where my father died. Sam was truly a comfort to Dave. Sam got up on his chest and nibbled Dave's chin. He slept curled up by him and Dave would rest his hand on Sam's warm fur. Sam went in and out the door at the foot of Dave's bed. Dave would say—Sam wants in! Sam wants out!

My brother carried on with living and dying for exactly a month after we got him home from the hospital. Early in that time, I made a mad dash back to New Mexico to fetch my own cat who I'd had to board in a kennel for a couple of weeks. I'd promised Dave that I'd take Sam home with me and we started working on introducing the cats to each other. Not a smooth operation. Sam was much older, bigger, and had a lot more attitude. It was his territory too. But we tried; spitting, chasing, hissing cats, one on each side of a baby gate. I got some cat pheromones from the vet and we were all steeped in cat pheromones for weeks.

When my brother died one cold mid-morning. Sam was there too. With the help of the hospice nurse, Thomas, my brother Ray and I cleaned Dave's body and got him dressed, (one can't meet the ancestors with no pants). We shrouded his body, sprinkled him with rose buds and juniper, and waited for the funeral home folks to come take his body for cremation. Sam lay on Dave's legs until they took Dave away.

After Dave's funeral, I drove back cross country in late winter. My SUV was packed to the gills with tools and dishes from my brother and I was carrying two mewling cats. Due to weather, it took me four days. It seemed to be going pretty well—neutral territory in the motels—cat pheromones plugged into the wall socket each evening. Even I wanted to curl up and knead.

We made it home and the boys were getting along alright. My home is only 250 square feet, I have no interior doors, and I'll have to admit there were a lot of scuffles. Sam was dominate here too, and my cat, Tangus, was intimidated much of the time. Sam was getting older, had trouble climbing the ladder to the loft, was losing his teeth. We did many alternating ins and outs, I broke up lots of small fights, and they always got food and goodies at the same time. Because we have hungry coyotes and bobcats around, I tried to alternate Sam and Tangus in the small catio I'd built. Sam, however, was a real Houdini and wouldn't stay in. I could see him wondering, where is Dave, and why is this difficult woman always trying to confine me?!

I was bringing the cats in for the evening a couple of months into our new arrangement. It was dusk, and I carried Tangus from the catio to the house. Then went back out to call Sam in. He'd been near the car in the yard when I brought Tangus in. I called him but he didn't come. I looked all around, calling, but no Sam. I went out looking every couple of hours all through the night, but no Sam. I went to my neighbor's house in the early morning to see if Sam was there. No Sam. No Sam. No Sam.

I was crying and crying. The bobcat comes near our houses. The coyote does too. I felt like I'd failed my brother, failed to keep Sam safe, failed, failed, failed.

Later that morning I was looking out the window, still hoping Sam might return. I noticed a large white-winged dove wandering around the yard. It was waddling near the porch steps, then would wander back towards the garden. I've never seen a white-winged dove here. It was alone too, an oddity for a dove. I immediately thought of Sam.

I looked up meanings for the sighting of a dove. "The dove is a symbol of the soul's release from its earth-bound duty. It symbolizes peace of the deepest kind. It soothes worried or troubled thoughts."

The dove was there just that one morning, I've not seen it again.

Sometimes I think there are extraordinary agreements made. Agreements between aging cats who have lost their favorite person and hungry bobcats. I hope so. I hope Sam is snuggled with my brother, nibbling on his chin and lying on his legs.

The week after Sam disappeared, I spooked up a bobcat in the cholla when I took my loop walk. As I watched the bobcat run, full-out across the desert, I glimpsed Sam's body overlaid on the bobcat's sleek form: incorporated, transmuted, integrated, joined.

Dave, Sam, the bobcat, me, you. Who can comprehend the disremembered obligations we may have agreed to? Life, death, the choices we seem to make. Destiny, luck, consequence. Stories of doves and bobcat-agreements may just be pretexts and justifications, a lame way to make myself feel better. I still choose it. I choose mystery over randomness.

Dissolution

Excavations:
Garage Archaeology Field Notes

I'm doing ground reconnaissance, a surface survey. On top the site is littered with fragments of divorce debitage: receipts for lawyer's fees, decrees and drafts of decrees, real estate contracts. I tune in and sift the atmosphere, the ambiance. Yes . . . shattered dreams, wounded hearts. The anguish is everywhere, a layer a few inches thick covers everything. There is evidence of extensive tear-flow—runnels and spattering—salt residue.

I dig below that surface stratum. There are narratives here, laid in long ago and stored like a cache of flint cores. I open a box, just one square of data in the context of this excavation. I find an assemblage of mixed items: notes and cards, a doll, old leather-bound books, refrigerator magnets, house plans, small framed photos, unframed photos, a few office supplies. The layers take me back in time to a different culture, a different structure.

There is the evidence, incontrovertible. The hand-written love notes, the photos of people with smiling eyes, documentable project collaborations, the building of homes, shared ideals, a good life; it was present once. Real. The chronology of the box substantiates the *existence of love—verifies past love.*

As in all excavations, the collections, the artifacts, the clues, create more questions than they answer. Where did the shift happen along the timeline? What were the influences, the pressures? What forces were at work internally, externally; love-erosion, frost-wedging-hearts, climactic-shifting-dreams?

Perhaps what this project needs is an extensive use-wear analysis. But the matrix is now destroyed. Nothing in situ.

Tactical Retreat

the energy of the summer desert is retreat
divine withdrawal
a tactical contraction

the sun
high, white, brilliant

makes the shadow's essence
seek refuge under the stone
and the wise snake finds the burrow

the sun
strong, severe, insistent

makes the substance of the cloud
vanish like the single drop of dew that materialized
in the night
the shrewd raven hunts out the deep crevice
on the canyon's north side
and calls over and over again to his god

this life
this time
now
is like the sun
intense, harsh, relentless

instinct tells you to shelter
like rabbit in the barely moist hollow
like javelina in dappled mesquite shade
like quail scratching for dampness in the dry wash

like badger gone to ground
you wish to be surrounded by rootlets and cool stones and silence

the glare, the stark light, is too much
the gritty sand abrades
the salty sweat stings

instinct helps you remember

you evoke the spirit of the spade foot toad
who three feet under the parched sand
inhabits real stillness

the wait does not consist of faith in future rain
but only of toad-presence in dark moist soil
long holy retreat

3

Unhoused

John O'Donohue, the Irish poet and teacher, says that suffering unhouses us; takes us unwillingly out of the familiar and the safe. He says that when we become unhoused the first things that leave us are meaning and belonging. Amen, John.

I would say that I'm suffering right now, yes, but small "s" suffering compared to what could be. I'm definitely navigating the geography of loss, crossing the transition bridge, feeling set adrift in a small boat on a deep dark sea.

And I'm missing the anchor of meaning and belonging. Capital "M". Capital "B".

In the last month, through chiefly my own choices, I've divorced after twenty-some years, resigned from my job, graduated my daughter from University and right out of the nest, sold my house, and temporarily left the west. I've gone from 100 miles per hour to zero in the obligations department, have nowhere in particular to go every day, and only Sam, my cat, to care for, and he doesn't even make piles of laundry.

So, a woman has got to ask herself at this point in time, why am I here on planet Earth and where do I belong? Those are the unsolved mysteries ahead of me. I'm trying to relax into this place of unknowing; float a little while in that small boat on the deep dark sea and watch for friendly dolphins as opposed to sea monsters. I'm holding the intention to just be still after the last few years and breathe. Breathe and do nothing. Breathe and let the heart in me rise.

On my walks here on the family farm in Ohio, where I've taken short-term refuge, I've been noticing lots of wild grape vines. They range up the trees like they know where they're going. I admire their tendrils, tips like thin alien fingers reaching for the next thing to grasp.

Maybe my soul is like those tendrils, stretching toward the next solid thing to hold onto, acting as if it knows where it's going even if I don't, heading up, up, searching for a place to unfold in the light.

4

Truth Telling

My all-time favorite job interview question was, "How do you feel about being a pariah?" The outfit I ended up working for did a lot of ground-truthing logging and mining sites and watch-dogging government agencies. Exposing truth, looking for truth in the dog pile, it's outsider work, outcast work. Park-your-car-in-lighted-places work.

We learn as children, and are reaffirmed as adults, that telling the truth can be dangerous. It's a double standard thing. We're supposed to hold truth telling at the highest value, but the daily role modeling totally falls short of the mark.

Probably my toughest life lessons to date have revolved around speaking truth to power in public and truth to power in intimate situations. I've had to struggle mightily with my internal sissy; screwing up the courage, fortitude, and fearlessness required to shake in my boots and still say it out loud.

Nobody in power likes a truth teller, and the rest of us admire truth tellers in silence or in secret behind-closed-doors gratitude sessions. *Wow! I'm so glad you said what everyone was thinking.*

If you speak truth consistently, you'll accidentally become a representative for the unwilling or unable to speak. Truth telling is treacherous but necessary. And really, really, scary to do alone.

Truth telling ends up being soul-stuff and spine-stuff. In this corporeal political world, the results of truth telling can be harsh indeed, my dear pariah. Called on the mat, pariah. Pulled off the management team, pariah. Divorced, pariah. But at least you can look in the mirror. The bell of your soul rings true. What people find in your eyes is clean and trustworthy.

5

Things Imagined and Uncared For

I think the deepest pain we feel in loss is the loss of potential. We dwell on the what-could-have-beens and what-should-have-beens and know it's too late. The aching is keen, sharp-edged and jagged.

In his lovely early book, *River Notes*, Barry Lopez describes what might be the source of rivers. He tells of grieving ravens up in the headwaters, mourning losses, so very many losses, and crying dark fat tears. One of the things they grieve for is "the loss of what is imagined, but uncared for." Yes. All those plans. All those intentions. All that lost tenderness and care.

The road from what was sweet and kindhearted swerves and bends and we somehow find ourselves in a pothole as big as Texas, with a broken axel and an empty gas tank. We sit there on the roadside, a crumpled, creased, coffee stained map in our laps, and wonder how the hell we got there. When did our attention flag? When did the weather change? How can we look into those familiar eyes we've been riding along with for more than twenty years and see an unhappy stranger?

How long have we been sleeping? We suddenly wake up one day at the bottom of a splitting fissure. What was shiny and lovely and magical over time gets dents and scratches. We stop tending. We don't wash things off or polish the surface. Things oxidize and we stop seeing the true color. We live in a greying haze. We slowly settle into valuing functionality more than joy. Dinner's ready. Taxes paid. Work comes early in the morning, we're tired and distracted at night.

At the beginning we imagined this could never happen *and yet it did*. It does. An uncared-for love dulls and fades. Then seemingly out of the blue, surprises us, asleep at the wheel, with its incremental departure.

This familiar process, this sad pattern we humans repeat, causes me to wonder what it is in our characters that makes us consistently fall short.

How is it that we can understand what makes the ravens weep and yet can't seem to stop it, to change it, to see it coming, to modify our way. *It's absolutely everywhere, this pattern of not tending to the things we say we love the most.* Each other, the earth, our own weary souls.

I sense one dark round tear after another running down my face. I feel the need to be near a river, at the headwaters.

6

Labyrinth Walk in Monsoon Season

Just now
I steadfastly desire silence, solitude, and vistas
the company of those whose path we have not altered—
lizard, snake, songbird, spider, the tiny blue butterfly on a papery white flower.

Trying to ground,
orange blooms on barrel cactus
put me in mind of California poppies—I am powerfully drawn to their color.
I would curl up inside a bloom as rusty as a fox and as fiery as Mars
if I could.
Absorb the long wave lengths of light
until my soul uncurled, relaxed,
becoming its own velvety sunflower-marigold petal
beckoning bees like the muse.

In the center I stand
feel the heat rise up off the slab
let myself receive the undulating landscape
gratefully accept the presence of prickly pear, palo verde, saguaro and greasewood and cholla.
The escarpment in the distance is a sheltering garden wall.

The stone bench at the exit-entrance is as hot and soothing as a sauna.
Sitting now, not focused on seeing after walking the circuits
a single vulture catches my eye.
He circles the stormy sky above the labyrinth once
then drifts off toward the mountains tilting on the bumpy air.

Just now
there is rain there
falling in a misty sheet as beautiful and dear
in the desert as an aurora.

Vulture brings me a message.
Pare to clean bone.
Let the sun purify the white austerity of nothingness—and dwell there.
Tenderly let yourself ride some unseen current
into a surprising sweep of sweet water.
Allow nurturing veils to descend like magic in the desiccated landscape of heart.

Vulture lives each day in elemental trust.
In fundamental patience.

In solidarity, my companion.

7

Care

It started with Kim. A sort of recognition or resonance. We were in the Atlanta airport just chatting to kill time. I was explaining my dream of putting together a survey course on staying human. She said the ideas gave her goosebumps and then she asked me, "Do you know what I dream about doing? I want to take care of people like you who are working to help the world. You are like a human treasure."

A human treasure. The words *take care of* were what really got me. I got choked up and couldn't talk. *To be cared for by someone, viewed as a human treasure.* Wow! Care. It seems like it should be such a daily thing, something expected, taken for granted. A wise woman I know says to pay attention to your tears, they'll unerringly signal the potent things. I started thinking about why that small exchange, with a person I don't know well, hit me with such force.

I was up on the mesa in Sky City. There was a nice Acoma man, a pen and ink artist. He was flirting with me in a gentle slow way. He noticed my Celtic triple spiral tattoo and asked me what that symbol means in my culture. I was explaining the triple goddess, the movement of the worlds, the circle that is the cauldron of transformation, and he reached over so tenderly and brushed my hair away from the tattoo. In that plain, non-very-meaningful moment, as he touched my shoulder and told me that the Acoma have the same symbol, but it represents the winds, I felt that recognition and resonance again. *Care.* I wanted someone in my life to touch me with that kind of gentleness. That tiny tender motion, a brushing away, a kindness speaking in the eyes. I suddenly knew. *That's what's missing.* The lack of feeling cared for is what brings me to tears.

Ah. The solving of a mystery, funny little puzzle pieces clicking together like magnets. Slowly becoming aware of the incremental way we crust over and stop even noticing that we're starving to death. How does it happen? How does intimacy curdle into hardness and withholding?

There are lessons here I know. Lessons about how to live and love. About facing fear. About

76

dysfunctional long-term coping patterns. About realizing what kind of a dance partner you've been.

Maybe I'm beginning to understand again what I want, what I need. Maybe I'm learning to courageously expose the bleeding heart lying on my knees. If that bloody mass makes you turn away, well then, I'll start again. Life is too short to live without care or tenderness. I'm a human treasure and so are you.

8

The Iterative Nature of Grief

gain. A slow creep of cold condenses around my heart, turns it to stone. It's like the sky darkening, blue to black, like blood soaking through gauze, like the purpling of a bruise. It's a quiet thing, a persistent thing. I find myself looking up from my reading, my mind ensnared. I lay the book open on my knee. The book, my heart, the day, have all become unbearably heavy. I stare. I sigh.

It's over and done. A year's gone by. There's no going back. I *know* that. No reset. No reparation. That world is gone, gone, gone. Yet I replay the days. Reanalyze my reactions, my decisions—as if it still mattered—as if there's some purpose in repeating the process. Once the tilt happens and the waters rise, I can't seem to stop the cascade. Guilt, failure, and remorse settle out like gravel from a flood pulse, gritty, sharp and abrasive.

I literally spend days wondering if I should reach out and send a birthday card. It feels like détente, with all the inherent risks and dangers.

Distance and time passing makes everything even stranger, clarity increases in some places and gets turbid in others. The way things unwound continues to boggle, makes me shake my head and wonder. How do these things happen? How do these implausible things happen?

There are a thousand jagged edges that need to be ground smooth. They still cut deep if I drag my soul along them. Maybe the iterative nature of grief, the again-ness of it, the need to reexamine, to repeat, is like grinding stone against stone.

Someday after uncounted scraping circles—of going around and around and around—there will be smoothness, polish, luster. Someday, a stone will be burnished, the jagged edges, the imperfections, the sharpnesses, worn away. That will be a thing worthy of holding.

9

A Letter from My Ex-Husband

Even three years on, I react strongly to his handwriting. I drive to the post office planning my afternoon, feeling settled, the drive along the Chama now normal and familiar. My mind is idling along. I'll pick up the books I know are in my post office box, refill my drinking water containers at the general store across the street, then head home to my cat and the drums I left drying in the studio. But along with the book packages and the junk mail circulars there is a business size envelope. I instantly recognize the hand.

I'm amazed really, how my body kicks in at just the sight. An adrenaline rush materializes, my heart rate climbs, and the well-known elephant's foot settles in the center of my chest. It's a queer combination; predominately fear with a quirky undercurrent of hopefulness.

I'm afraid to open it. My rational mind is saying, relax, it's just about divorce details, he only contacts you once a year about money, but my "I-was-entwined-with-this-person-for-twenty-five-years" mind is screeching. It's wringing its hands and hoping there isn't something absolutely excoriating in there. It's gone chalk-white, its mouth dry, terrified some deeply triggering language will throw ice water on its very heart-and-soul. And at the same time, and this is truly the alarming part, my "I-was-entwined-with-this-person-for-twenty-five-years" mind is hopeful that maybe there will be something conciliatory in there. Maybe something kind and peacemaking. Dear Susan, it might say. It could contain condolences or maybe forgiveness. Perhaps even something like an expression of regret.

I stack up my packages and wrap the letter inside the ads. I joke with the gentle post office ladies. I go fill my three-gallon carboys. I drive home along the Chama, through the red rock and the harsh sunlight. The whole way back my heart is tight and aching, and I allow my mind to bounce between its fear and its hope. Fear and hope. Fear and hope. That other part of my brain, the reasonable part, the part that went to some university, is chanting in the background, it's just about money, it's just about money.

I clatter and rock along the final four miles of bad New Mexico road staying distracted,

79

way up in my head; fear and hope, it's just about money. I pull the Ford onto the gravel patch under the juniper. Wild sunflowers are blooming across my yard. They make me happy, those yellow flowers, they really do.

I change out the water jug, open my book packages and read the flyleaves. I throw the junk mail in the recycle bin. I sigh. I screw up my courage. I take the business sized envelope with my ex-husband's penciled writing on it out to my table in the studio. I sit down. I open it.

My heart rate slows down and my fear eases. Distressingly, my heart also breaks. It's just a few terse lines. About money.

10

Herons & Venus Retrograde

Herons.
Herons in flight, low across water
or herons standing immersed-branch still.
Herons high,
wing spans so wide for a second a soul might think, golden eagle—
but no, see the legs dangling, the curved-back-on-itself neck?

One heron drops a flight feather on the water,
perfect grey-blue, twice as long as an extended hand.
A magical gift, a joy.
A memory forms then, a quiet lake in Oregon,
gathering feathers floating on the flat surface from a canoe,
a preening heron in the Sitka above—
later, grey-blue feathers lovingly placed inside a well-used yellow-faced guitar.
They may still be there.

Venus is retrograde, backtracking, reviewing.
Herons are flying over dry New Mexico,
reflected in the receding water,
contrasting with the red rock.
In the pouring rain along Loch Fyne,
they come even closer, hunching on black rock, battered by the weather,
gentle gargoyles.
Messengers.
Totems from the past.

Venus is retrograde,
for weeks now traveling back through the arc of the zodiac.
Herons continue flying over wherever I am.
I imagine them
carrying tarot cards hidden in their feathers—3 of swords, 5 of cups.
The 10 of swords, ruin, love lost, endings, borne in a sharp stabbing beak.
Venus drifts backward, taking her time.
A heron wades slowly in the shallows, then stills.

It's cold now, and snowing.
Argyll far, far away.
The lake is so low, icy, and as blue-grey as a heron feather.
No visits to the waters lately.

Herons?
They may still be there.

11

Reflections on My Daughter's 25th Birthday

Twenty-five years ago.

Even then love was perilous.
Reckless and beautiful.
What was sure?
My tight stretched belly.
The hawk in the tree.

The lures were strong. Siren songs. Pheromones.
Hard to resist. Impossible maybe.
Archetypal dances,
karmic attractions, debts, lessons.
Dreams dense with messages and wrapped in symbols.

Who knows what we were working on—
working out—
being worked by.

I loved you.
It was magnetic, the draw. Elemental. Fey-spell potent.
There was Merlin in the shadows.
I could sense the crone, her steady eye on me at the center of a pulling gyre.
You drew the Ace of Cups, the Empress.
Ripe and willing, I stepped into the turning circle,
an impetuous combination of glowing heart,
powerful powerlessness, and trust trying like a twining vine,
tendrils seeking sun and support.

Twenty-five years ago, today.
The hawk in the tree.
The seals in my dreams.
Waiting, walking, worrying.

Those early days
when you'd disappear all day walking—confused and muddled,
you were married still, after all,
my trepidation would grow.
I'd whisper promises to that tight stretched belly.
Murmur secret promises of care, care, care.
No matter what.
No matter what—forever shelter, protection.
Utters of mother-love as dense as basalt
and as deep as the ocean.
A kit curled in my womb
slick and small,
tumbling and turning like a seal.
I loved her.

I loved you.
I remember, exactly.
Sweet and fierce and complex and crazy.
Sure and unsure. Turbulent and tender.

When she was coming, moving slowly down the birth canal,
I leaned against you, groan-growling—transformed into a feral bear-woman,
I shuffled around, in a cave-deep dream, rumble-roaring.
Squatting in labor, inhabiting the otherworld of birthing,
pulling on your hands, your arms, there was nothing else
known to hold on to.

You loved her instantly and, in the exhilaration,
me.
Even from my blur I could sense that.
Felt love like the heat from a fire.
Fragile and gentle, warm, kind.
For those moments,
father, mother, child.
A trinity, a unity.

You cradled her head in your palm.
Small as a cat, that one,
slick as a seal.

So, what was sure?
The hawk in the tree
bringing the news of her coming.

What is sure?
Love is never just one thing.

Love is beauty and peril.
Forever and not.
Fierce and tender.
Sure and uncertain.

What is sure, you ask me?
I would have to say,
just that one thing.

Pilgrimage

1

Surprising Pilgrimage

Praying All Over

I pinned on the scallop shell and set out on the weary road.

I was exceedingly hollow, like the dark world before anything came, like the void before the first cell's division. In every direction only obsidian ripples, a long fetch, just open distance for the cold indifferent wind to howl across. Like the man who loved Bridget O'Malley, my heart was a stone. My soul felt blown, wrecked, imploded. It sounds overly dramatic, but when you're in that space, the emptiness and lack of purpose is utterly, profoundly, undeniably real.

Dissolution leaves you teetering on the precipice of a bottomless pit, sensing with certainty that below you lies a gravity-sucking black hole. Loss. The maw wants filled, and you are empty, gift-less, bare, without a single resource. It feels massive. Immoveable. Dense. The endless weary road stretches before you. An unbidden pilgrimage begins.

Even embedded in that density, that dispirited place of being locked naked inside a cold black stone, a kernel-like thing deep inside you urges, *move. Just move.* Take tiny steps. Keep breathing. Pray without ceasing.

Movement becomes a blessing then, the unceasing prayer. Being in motion gives meaning to the empty hours and days. The kernel-like thing says listen, listen for where you are meant to go. Load your pack with essentials: maps, invocations, humility, the metaphorical scallop shell.

For a while you drag along the empty calcified shell that was your old life, afraid to put it down lest you disappear altogether. For a while you are burdened not only with your pilgrim's pack filled with essentials, but with an old identity, a worn-out way, outdated thoughts. In the years of chosen homelessness, like a monk with an empty bowl, I prayed.

I prayed for my family that was no longer a family. I prayed for our best good, our highest purpose. For healing. For insight. I prayed for myself, that I might learn from this detonation, somehow become a better person. I prayed that through the process of moving, I'd become stronger, wiser, more compassionate. I prayed for forgiveness for my unconscious mistakes and

89

for my conscious ones. I prayed to be able to forgive others. I prayed for new direction. I prayed for modest glimmers of light.

In those years of chosen homelessness, I prayed in many places.

I wrote petitions on scraps of paper and left them in the basket altar in the chapel on Iona. I left coins and clooties at holy wells in Cornwall. I spoke my best truth among my sisters, seen and unseen, in the roundhouse on Dartmoor. I laved myself in the red waters of the Chalice Spring. I blended the waters from the white spring and the red spring and drank them every day for a week. In honor of the goddess and women, I ate windfall apples from the orchards on the side of Glastonbury Tor. I walked sunwise around stone circles older than old. I sat silent in burial chambers, fogous, and quoits and asked my ancestors for guidance. I gazed with reverence and awe into cysts and barrows built by ancient ancestors.

I wrote old, new, unresolved, and unspoken griefs on paper. On a secluded white sand beach, I bound them to rocks and threw them as far out to sea as I could. I called to the seals, my selkie sisters, for help finding my lost pelt. I meditated every day in community. I cooked, cut wood, shared stories, explored, and gardened with my adopted family on Erraid.

I splashed my prayerful face with the miracle waters of Apache Spring. I buried quartz crystals in the directional quarters of the Ohio garden and contemplated inside for months. I appealed to the spirits on a New Mexico mesa top surrounded by red-rock and pot sherds and received a song. I quested alone on a tiny island in the Alladale River, swirled around by water and wind and my own thoughts. I did the same search two years on, on an unnamed island off the Ross of Kintyre, following the sunlight with my face like a plant and feeling for the future.

In those years of chosen homelessness, I moved and moved and moved.

For some remarkable years I was a wanderer. I wore the scallop shell. I carried the empty bowl. I was often sustained and buoyed by friends and family. I learned, absorbed, made new friends, and studied beautiful landscapes. I slowly scraped away pieces of old exoskeleton, old identity, old ways, old thoughts. The black void gradually filled with adventure, new-found-strengths, different perspectives, ancestors, a love for solitary travel. That kernel-like thing still advises listening and movement.

I've settled, like an ocean-borne larva, at least for now. I'm appreciating having a home base again and enjoying the illusion of permanence a house and land bring. In some ways it feels good to be investing in a specific place. I like developing gardens and learning the patterns of weather. I always aspire to understanding the life cycles of the creatures and plants that share the landscape. I take pleasure in watching, from a single point, the light and vegetation change as the days and seasons flow by.

I'm restless though, crave movement. I wake up listening. I'm still unsure of my ultimate destination.

2

Slick-Rock

It's about trust, really.
Imagining the next rock cairn will appear.
It's not certainty exactly,
but tender cultivation of a timid willingness to assume
one is being led in the right direction.

Leaving with no map, just nebulous descriptions,
one ought to set off with a conviction that
just over that slick-rock rise
there will be a signal—
and then another.
The obligation of doubt must be set aside
for the hope of a silhouette of stone.

It's about trust, really,
Trading ground truthing theories
for faith.
Heart-believing the path before us is marked by some hand.
Knowing in the deepness of your soul that a sign will materialize
when it's needed.

The vivid yellow flowers, pungent sage, and periwinkle lichen
are gifts along the way.
So too the stark landscape, the flat-bottomed clouds, the whole silence.

See there? Another cairn.

3

Sonoran Desert to Deciduous Forest

On the days-long drive, the image that keeps rising in my mind is of clean bone, dry bone, with creeping tendrils of moss just beginning to cover it. In my mind I see damp forest litter, dry bone, am a witness to the slow absorption of a dead framework, a partial skeleton. There's an enigmatic neutrality in the image: good, bad, who can say what's what with dissolution? With being undone.

There is a dramatic softening of the landscape going east, a continually building unfocused quality, the blurring of edges. Much is hidden. There is an aggressive abundance of growth, decay, vapors. Everything is bright green, kelly green, an abnormal startling green to my desert eyes. The shoulders of the rolling hills are shrouded in graceful fogs of a morning, the world loudly buzzing with insects.

It feels foreign, exotic, disorienting. Just as the beginning of a pilgrimage should be.

I must let go of my cherished love of the merciless light, the crisp shadows, the dry clean bone. The lack of decomposition. Who am I now in this strange geography? Am I simply inert dissolving minerals or an embodiment of the reaching green?

With time, what does moss make of bone?

4

Reviving Artemis

In her book, *Artemis: The Indomitable Spirit in Everywoman*, Jean Shinoda Bolen describes Artemis as one of the three virgin goddesses of Greek mythology. She states that the virgin-goddess-archetype represents the part of a woman that is unowned by a man or a need to be validated by him. Artemis exists separate from a man and lives untouched by masculine collective opinion. Bolen goes on to say that Artemis can live happily in the privacy of a woman's inner life, moved to action by her own motivations and desires.

I'm reviving Artemis.

I'm taking on the process of rediscovering who I might be in the context of the privacy of my woman's inner life.

I have always been drawn to the symbols of Artemis, the wild animals, the wilderness, the silver bow, the moon. But like many women, I put aside the independence and free-thinking of Artemis when I partnered with husbands and adapted to our cultural norms in schooling, work, and domestic life.

In my sixties now, Artemis the Bear is beckoning, the Deer, the bow. I've stumbled into the metaphorical wilderness of major life transition. Calling on Artemis, I'm cultivating an attitude that transmutes loss and disorientation into an opportunity to reinvent, renew, recalibrate, review, and remember.

Artemis loves the natural world and being out in it. She enjoys a sisterhood of women, traveling with her nature-nymphs, and acts decisively to protect other women, children, animals, and Gaia herself. Artemis enjoys her own company and her own interests. Artemis cares deeply about fairness and can flow forthrightly into rage and retribution. Artemis speaks truth to power and loves an intellectual challenge. Artemis follows a path with heart.

So, dear Artemis, I call to you. Bear-mother protectress, avenging boar, wandering-the-wilderness deer, sister-companion, I call to you.

Recently, I've obtained a bow.

5

The Color Orange

I've found myself very attracted to the color orange for the last few years. Pure California poppy orange, Sedona red-rock orange, butterfly wing orange, and right now, daylily-in-every-ditch orange. I would love to just crawl into one of the blooms and wrap myself like a pupa in that siren-call color. The daylily color is richest and purest viewed under about-to-rain cloud cover in late afternoon light. Saturated, intense, soul penetrating.

I believe that colors are like foods. We crave them we somehow need them at a cellular level. I believe that color is healing and therapeutic. So, ORANGE!

I looked up color meanings for orange and here are some of the quotes that resonated with me as I read through.

Orange offers emotional strength in difficult times. It helps us to bounce back from disappointments and despair, assisting in recovery from grief. The color psychology of orange is optimistic and uplifting, rejuvenating our spirit. Orange brings spontaneity and a positive outlook on life. With its enthusiasm for life, the color orange relates to adventure and risk-taking, inspiring physical confidence, competition and independence.

Orange aids in the assimilation of new ideas and frees the spirit of its limitations, giving us the freedom to be ourselves. At the same time, it encourages self-respect and respect of others.

Well, wow, orange!

And from another site: *Healing properties: Orange is warm, cheering, non-constricting. Orange has a freeing action upon the body and mind, relieving repressions. Orange shows new possibilities and other options in life. A preference for orange: Orange represents the warmth of the fire. It represents celebration and great abundance, comfort, enjoyment of the senses. Orange appeals to warm, sociable, dynamic and independent people who dedicate themselves to whatever they do.*

Now I'm thinking of it as Artemis Orange! It seems the perfect color for the times.

Zinnia, marigold, lily, squirrel back, begonia, Monarch, robin breast, terra cotta clay. Think of me next time you peel an orange. Zest!

6

Chaco Canyon Pilgrimage

There must be distance
and discomfort,
a stark white light to peel away illusion
and flatten shadow.
There must be silence
broken only by lizard-skitters, raven-knocks, and wind.
You must be alone.

Even as you leave a comfortable home
in your well-tuned car
your cell phone charged,
your cooler full of apples and cheeses—
in your heart
you won't feel sure that you will get there,
or return.

There is distance, hours spent driving.
Circles of thought swirl and form like
monsoon clouds building on an unfamiliar horizon.
The map seems confusing—no road signs appear—
turn right or left at White Horse?

Dust piles up on the windscreens.

There is evidence of flooding,
dried splays of red mud beside deep ruts,

no one comes from the direction you are going.

Coyote greets you, but looking over his shoulder
and tucking tail he runs away.

When you fell into a restless sleep
in the hot afternoon
the sky was clear.
You may have come seeking insight from the stars—
but receive word from lightning.
Black clouds frame Fajada Butte.
Thunder calls mix with the cricket song.
Wind whirls the sparse leaves
on the single tree you sit beside
and dances the creosote bushes.
Pink lightening veins slate-blue clouds.
In the distance there is rain.

You think about the ancestors,
all the things they knew that you don't.
You wonder about the ones
who pecked the spiral high on the butte
and about the ones that elbowed the slabs in place
to create daggers of light.

If all goes well, tomorrow you'll make a prayer.

On the slick-rock above the canyon
facing South Gap
you orient your face to the sun.
It takes time.
You wait for the feeling of being rooted

all the way to the center of the earth to settle over you.

The silence itself is a prayer.
The white light on your face an invocation.

Ancestor Women on the right,
Ancestor Men on the left.
They extend back into time, into wholeness
and then oneness.

You realize in this life you are the point of a spear.

All you can do
is invite guidance and seek forgiveness.
On the hard rock you long to be heard.
In the stark light you yearn for compassion.
In intact silence you crave their benevolence, tenderness, gentleness, kindness.
If it comes
you pass it on as a gift.

When you started early
nine vultures perched in the cottonwoods.
They hung their strong black wings like sodden cloaks
in the morning coolness.

Now they fly.

UK Haiku

Eastbound raven flight
Miles of sea, miles of distance
Hope rides on black wings

8

September on Erraid

My hands are sticky with resins from gathering cooking herbs. When I make my tea for morning break, I smell the rosemary and sage. When I brush back the tendrils of hair loosened by the wind, I smell rosemary and sage.

I look out over granite block walls, past the fuchsia hedge, to the bays and stacks between here and Iona. Blue as lapis today. The small ferry makes another run. The Abbey sits huge and grey to the right of the cluster of white shops and hotels and houses on Iona.

I'm in charge of making the week's bouquets. I wander around the gardens looking for yellow flowers to compliment the sprays of wormwood I start with. The small bumble bees keep me from choosing this bloom or that one; they look so intent. One bee lands on the flowers I've gathered and rides along with me for a while, its little black head dusted with pollen.

I hear the others at their jobs, Matt working on glazing a window, Julia and Marissa picking the late crop of peas. I smell soup cooking in the kitchen. Now and then I hear a sheep baa, or the chickens set up a ruckus. A few songbirds scatter sweet notes in the willow trees and off towards the beaches the ravens caw. The wind blows strands of hair across my face again. As I smooth it out of my eyes with my resin-coated hands, I smell rosemary and sage.

Scars Precious and Rare

The card that I drew that morning was "healing". Let your woundedness go, it advised.

Old Bruce Cockburn song lyrics came to mind— "I've been cut by the beauty of jagged mountains. I carry these scars precious and rare."

The weeks progress and each morning before work, we blow out the meditation candle. Each morning the question is asked; Does anyone have someone to send the light to? In my mind, I quietly send the light to my own heart. I privately pray for its healing. Maybe it's alright to be selfish in this way. Maybe it's time.

Most days I feel a tightness around my heart, a constriction. If I tried to describe it to you, I'd say it's like a binding. Like something wrapped in morning glory vines made of steel, or like a wood carving project held in a vice. Or maybe I would tell you my heart's become less elastic like over-kneaded dough, welted with scar tissue that doesn't stretch. It's a fist that can't relax.

I lay my palm across it. The warmth of my hand soothes.

I carry these scars precious and rare. Let your woundedness go.

One morning in the mediation room, high above the inlet, I had an image come. Triggered, I think, by a poem I heard just once so long ago that most of it is gone; something about bees working in the heart. In the vision I saw my sore heart and on the darkened spots, over the bruises, honeybees were busy drawing comb. Bees produce wax in a magical process, transforming sugars into wax, secreting it between plates on their bellies; a small miracle of transmutation.

A small miracle. Transmutation. There on the damaged parts, around and between the healthy red, soft yellow bees are drawing comb, covering the abraded surfaces with creamy wax. They are loosening the bindings with a hundred tiny feet, affixing fresh multi-sided cells ready to receive sweet honey and bright pollen.

I've been cut by the beauty. Am a heart broken open. Mending, softening. I carry these scars, precious and rare. I'm letting the woundedness go.

If Only I Could Find My Pelt

In honor of our women ancestors and our female progeny, for all the women across time who have had their pelts stolen and concealed and for the ones who gave their sealskin away willingly once, and now miss it terribly.

The seals over through the Narrows are reliable. Every day they're there, suspended above the white sands in water rippling-clear and as blue-green as an old Mason jar. The shelf of the seafloor on this part of the island is a gentle slope. I know I could wade out into the cold flawless water, and if the seals would let me, I could, in waist-deep water, hold them in my arms.

Sisters, if only I could find my pelt.

Instead, I merely *imagine* embracing them. Imagine them singing a painfully beautiful seal-song of welcome home. Welcome home. They would swirl around my knees. Welcome home. They would lean back in the water, belly up, eyes wide. Our dear sister, welcome home.

I picture swimming with them as a seal-woman, out to the speckled sunning islet, hauling out onto the warm pink granite, resting on stone as old as our desire. I imagine living free in animal-joy, existing without forethought of trouble, immersed in the turquoise-water-moment, not fretting about the next storm. All yesterdays and tomorrows in abeyance.

Ah sisters, if only I could find my pelt.

I sit on the white sand, cockle shells and limpet shells and dried bits of kelp all around me. I smell iodine and rot and the faint lanolin-wet-wool of the black-faced sheep. *How is it, I think, that I'm still dried out like the kelp, still as empty as a cast up limpet shell?*

I feel the wind off the sea, feel the heat of the sun even through the wind, see the midnight-blue-turquoise-teal-grey-silver water change and change back with the shifting light. I hear the far-off creak of a sailboat's rigging. *How well hidden, I think, my sealskin is.* When I try to remember where I last saw it, the light shifts, the colors change. I am looking down into glass-clear-rippling water that distorts everything. I reach for that one reddish pebble in a foot of water—no, not quite where I reached—but just there—and, oops, now the waves have moved it. Covered it with sand.

I'm tired, I think, and lay back in the white sand. The top three inches are warm, but moisture wicks up through all the minute interstices in the sand matrix. I feel my clothes getting damp. *How well hidden, I think.* Maybe if I slept by the sea every day for a month, I would dream of the place my pelt is concealed. Maybe it's stuck in some black cave or icy crevice. Maybe it's rolled up and looking just like a rock, camouflaged unseen. Maybe it's lodged in the busted ribs of a shipwreck, my sealskin and the boat having both been caught off guard by grasping, sucking shoals.

The sun is low, and my ass is wet. I'm hungry, for sustenance and for human company, for companions. *It's time to go, I think, back to my cottage, pelt-less. Patience is a virtue, the soul is shy, takes a runner if you chase too hard, all things in their time, of course, and there are many tests of endurance, many, many tests.* I tell myself these things and try to believe them. I turn to the sea. Brush my hands together to dust away the sand. The tide has come up and the seals bob even closer, dog-like heads and round eyes watching me, watching them.

I call to my sisters, sister seals. Goodbye 'til tomorrow. Tomorrow we'll learn more. Tomorrow I'll dive in; naked, joyful, we'll swim together then. I'll find some trace tomorrow, I'm almost sure of it. I think, yes, surely tomorrow.

As I walk away, I pray to my sister seals, I call into myself their animal-joy, their sweet curiosity, their ability to gracefully ride the flow of the medium in which they live. Prayer-call into myself their calm-on-the-rocks, their instinct to dive and disappear, to come up far away from danger, their proficiency to *be*.

Farewell for today, I think. There will be discovery tomorrow. Surely tomorrow.

As I walk up the Narrows with the wind at my back, I see the rocky curve of the big island on the near horizon, on my right. As of this moment, the large and the small are joined. I smell wood-smoke and salt. The sandy bottoms of my jeans sandpaper the tops of my feet. *How is it, I wonder, that I am still so tender, that the sand, so soft and white, abrades my skin?*

Oh sisters, if only I could find my pelt.

11

Blackberry Communion

Cornwall. My mother's father's people come from here. I'm way south, not far from Penzance. I climb up into the moors, careful of abandoned tin-mine shafts, the sea and wind persistent companions.

Along the granite backbone of the peninsula there are no trees. The wind's too strong, the soil too infertile. The moors roll away, roll along, a dense tangle of heather, gorse, bracken ferns, and grasses. Nothing tall grows, the horizon broken only by occasional thrusts of bare rock. The moors are bleak but beautiful. Unpredictable winds mix up the clouds with the sky and dark shadows dart across the ground like ravens or harriers. Small mammals, maybe foxes, make smooth secretive tunnels under the dense growth. There's a sweet smell, floral, even though it's fall.

I'm relaxed but alert. I like the way the wind whips tendrils of hair around my face, the way it tugs at my clothes like a playful dog. I like this place. Cornwall. Alone and away, it speaks to me. I like how old things feel, as if time is a many-folded pirate's map. As if fierce nature spirits and powerful deities and tricky faeries and outlaw ghosts and land wights are wedged, ready to spring from every crack. It's lonely and wild. It feels spooky and slightly dangerous. One could get lost here. Really lost. There are holy places hidden all over it. Unfathomable, cryptic places.

I settle on a granite outcrop. Even exposed to the restless tussle of sea-wind, the sun is warm, the lee of the grey stones still. I gaze out over the green and grey and blue, and find myself thinking; *maybe I'm from here, in the same way I think sometimes I come from the stars.*

Time's quirky. I've been drifting in the granite energies. Woolgathering. Something makes me snap to. Suddenly the sedges in front of me are extra clear, crisp green sedges. My attention sharpens. Remember, I think; there are eerie places everywhere hereabout, long inhabited places.

My breath goes slow. I notice the tenderness of the rose-pink blooms along the vines. Note the intensely red-ochre shade the bracken has turned. Appreciate that the serrated and ridged leaves of the blackberry are turning purple and red even while still fruiting. And look, there in the concealing grasses, shining ripe blackberries. I gather a handful. Eat them. They're tart, sweet, clean.

Magical places. Inhabited places. Cornish blackberries. With full attention I eat something open and whole, the yield of this land. With intention, I ingest a creation ripened in an enchanted terrain, once the home of my ancestors. With this act I summon them, invoke them. I consume Cornish sun. Consume Cornish soil. Consume Cornish water. Consume moor-grown blackberries. They are the wafer in a holy communion.

12

Ambition and Bronze Age Pigs

I'm undone in so many ways. Unraveled. I feel myself straining like the curled tendril-tip on a vine, reaching toward something, anything; too tense, too expectant. Longing for something to clearly happen. I guess you can't count on synchronicity or manifestation or some other new age salvation coming to you just because you want it to. That must jinx it. Makes it take a runner. Sometimes I feel I'm called to teach but just what and to whom feels vague and slippery. I feel like I need a collaborative circle, a brain trust, a tribe, but don't seem to be finding a group to slot into, and don't feel the energy to start one. Sometimes I am so filled with excitement and ideas I can't sleep. Sometimes those same ideas seem stupid, lame, overworked and overdone and I'm so despairing of ever finding a new path and a new home that, guess what? I can't sleep.

I think I need to learn to let go. Really let go. To stop reaching. Become ambitionless. Let the currents drift me where they will and stop trying to paddle. Stop trying to read the texture of the water for signs. Is that land over there?! Do I smell fruit and soil?!

I'm feeling it deep in lately, a sense of just wanting to be somewhere still and have a quiet rhythm to the days. Monastic-lite. Sit by a sunny window, grow a few tomatoes on a little patio, let time flow unmeasured. No striving to sort life out or worse yet; *secretly hoping*. Holding a well-kept secret hope from my conscious self, for something specific (that vague and slippery teaching thing for instance). I keep remembering of one of Margaret Wheatley's fearless questions: Can you let go of needing to make a difference? I'm trying it out Margaret, giving it a go.

This week I got to visit with my friend Mara in Wales. We were on our way up to see some replicas of Bronze Age round houses and were chatting along the trail. I was mentioning this sense of feeling drawn to an ambitionless life and she remarked that she felt that too. She was saying that for both of us at our ages (sixty something) Saturn is below the horizon, and that causes an energy of drawing in and receiving instead of pushing out and producing. That's when we saw the pigs.

Two very content pigs, a breed as close to wild-to-domesticated Bronze Age pigs as modern breeders can make them. They were asleep under a hawthorn tree covered with red berries, curled tip ears twitching now and then. We watched them for a long time, amused and taken by their aura of complete serenity. They were sunning, covered in dry mud, eyes closed, forelegs relaxed, jowly cheeks resting on the raised edge of their nest. A perfect metaphor. I laughed and said those pigs embodied exactly how I want to be; ambitionless, content, comfortable in the moment, asleep in the sun cupped in a dusty bowl of clayish earth. They weren't surreptitiously reaching. They weren't trying to figure it all out.

In fact, as they dozed and stretched and grunted, they both seemed to be *smiling*.

13

How is the Universe Hinged?

an excerpt from a letter to C.J.

Life continues to be a wild ride with no settling down on a quiet plateau just yet. It's an uncomfortable space for a go-getter type, feeling very much suspended between stories, directionless and desiring direction, sometimes swamped with ideas and feelings of potentiality (feeling literally all wiggly inside, so full of unformed somethings it tickles). Sometimes scared there will be nothing substantive or meaningful ever again. Sometimes just physically exhausted and wanting nothing more than to sleep and sleep some more. I'm sure I'm following a typical pattern and feeling like anyone in these circumstances does. On a "pragmatic" level wanting to know where I'm going and to get there, *as quickly as possible.* I'm giving attention to resisting the urge to hurry through this process. Giving myself permission to just percolate a while, like ground water through interstices. To allow as long as it takes, I guess, even if that's a long time.

I'm appreciating the old chrysalis to butterfly metaphor and feel that right now I'm the dissolved mush before the imaginal cells start reshaping the little beastie into something new and completely different. During my last reading with Mara, she got lots of images of flight, birds wings and more birds. When I asked her toward the end of the reading what messages my guides had for me, she said they were laughing and putting on party angel wings and saying I was to put on my party wings and fly and have fun and sing my song. It would all be well.

There's a lot about trusting the universe to provide in there, and I'm working on that. Sometimes I still hear my mother's voice saying, "god helps those that help themselves." I used to have a quote on my wall, some cultural aphorism from somewhere, that said "call on god, but steer away from the rocks."

I think those axioms floating through my mind just now tell me that it is good to wait, to be patient, to not know, but at the same time you must prime the pump. Make yourself available.

Be condensation nuclei for cosmic collaboration. I think the universal flow wants a person to follow impulse and intuitive calls, to listen and be open, to pay attention, and to act. I want to learn to sense those subtle tugs and pulls and tip my craft into the currents at the right time, the best moment.

14

Attraction

a dream, then a letter . . .

After you left, I started thinking; what other thing is like this attraction? What could be a metaphor? An intermittent stream? The steadfast alignment of a compass needle to north? I think it's like telluric currents, meandering and subtle, barely detectable sometimes; ley lines crisscrossing the landscape of the heart. I wonder, pseudoscientist that I am, with rods, persistence, and discernment, could this feeling be dowsed?

There does seem to be a north-star-like constancy running through it, and apparently, it's immune to the passage of linear time. Evidence indicates that even after many years of geographic distance, lack of frequent communications, and plain old absence we're still drawn to each other. The pull is there. The dowsing rods tug downward when we cross paths.

The path, the ley, rambles though and disappears altogether at times. There are huge gaps in the mapping and an on-going sense of being somewhat ill-starred. We seem to never reach a node at the same time. The energy undulates in a wave form even longer than red light, longer than ELF radio waves.

Maybe what's good between us when we meet, the comfort and affection, the ease, the need to touch, flows from a past life as well-matched lovers, or issues from an ancient soul agreement, or if that new agey energy stuff is too much, we'll just say our link is an agreeable kind of plain, earthly love; simple, like water moving underground, which is the force that creates telluric currents to begin with.

Maybe love is always just a gift to be grateful for and not to analyze or gauge. Maybe Love, that enduring enigmatic power, gifts us with song-cousins, guardian angels, and star-crossed-almost-lovers merely to make us dwell in wonder once in a while.

So, I wonder.

I'm feeling my way forward from this strange place of dissolution where I live right now, fumbling out from the center of the blind spring that is my heart, my dowsing rods at the ready.

I want to verify a trace, check for signs that love indeed exists; that it's a real, if subtle, force on planet Earth. For these reasons I dowse. I bear witness to the blessing of companionship. I feel gratitude.

Gratitude that we shared some time and space, two parallel ley lines, pulled into congruence for a little while, creating an eddy of caring, innocent energy.

Your road takes you west, back to the rhythms of your life. My own road calls me far away, into some new pattern I can't predict, heeding a different kind of attraction altogether; another kind of pull.

As I walk away from where we stood, my dowsing rods swaying, I detect a ring of delicate energy. Several feet out, another even fainter one. I make note of it in my log. I'm attempting, ever so slowly, carefully, gently, to chart an unknown and indefinite terrain of the heart.

15

Are You Happy?

Excerpt from a letter to J.C.

I've been thinking about your questions since you asked them almost a week ago. *Are you happy? Do you have regrets?* In the moment, at that time, on the phone, I answered quickly; yes, I'm happier than I was, and of course I have regrets. And that answer was true. But my deeper answer, my "thinking-on-it-a-week" answer, is more complex and layered.

Hmmmm . . . where do we start? I guess the first thing that happened was that I started wondering about the very definition of "happy." I started asking myself; *was* I happy in my first marriage or my second? *Was* I happy in my work? Happy at all the different jobs and organizations over the last 40 years? *Was* I happy in my childhood? *Was I happy right now?* Do I know *anyone* who is happy?

Dictionary Definition of Happy:
delighted, pleased, or glad, as over a particular thing: *to be happy to see a person.*
1. characterized by or indicative of pleasure, contentment, or joy: *a happy mood; a happy frame of mind.*
2. favored by fortune; fortunate or lucky: *a happy, fruitful land.*

I guess, according to this definition, I'd have to say, so far in my life, in all situations, I have had *moments* of feeling happy.

However, those feelings of happiness are not sustained, continuous, or sometimes, even frequent. As I thought of others in my life, I concluded that this is pretty typical. An expectation of being happy as a ground-state was probably just setting ourselves up for disappointment. Moments of happiness: pleasure, contentment, delight, gladness, joy, these are transient things to be treasured when they come to us. Gifts. Little seashells and shooting stars. Secret kisses.

You know what questions I wish people would ask me?

Has your suffering made you more compassionate?
Have you learned to live with your regrets?
Will you behave differently in the future due to your experiences?

Those are tougher questions, and maybe the ones that matter most to me right now. Those are the questions I think we are consistently asked, not by our friends and family, but by the Universe, by Love, by whatever name you give to the Force of Creation. These are the questions that we must answer over and over and over again. A tough-love spiral, a virtuous cycle.

I guess all this blather is just to say I'm finding the cultivation of compassion more important than experiencing happiness. I guess I've come to believe all painful situations are lessons from the Universe and the curriculum is Love.

Don't think because of what I've said here that I don't want happiness, because I do. I want a sky full of it. I want it raining down on me and everyone I love. I want bouquets of it left on my doorstep. I want to give it away like cookies at Christmas. I want to find it written on a note in my lunch bag or tucked in my shoe.

Thanks for asking that question last week. It made me think. It made me write. It made me glad (see?! HAPPINESS) that I have so many lovely people in my life.

Raven Valentine

I've never liked Valentine's Day and its peculiar American sense of obligation and inadequacy. Like most "traditional" holidays here, it blares its commercial presence in the grocery, in the drug store, in the newspaper ads. I hate to admit that it affects me, even here in the place I've come to occupy, living marginalized on the edge of this queasy culture.

The pink and red flowery displays recall my circumstance; a drifting divorced woman, embedded in a dysfunctional family, society, world. It's all so inherently outlandish. And embarrassing really, I think to myself, *I should be so far past this.*

These were among my thoughts on February 14th, rolling toward the sea along the incredibly beautiful Smith River, wild still, and clean, even with the recent heavy rains. Mason-jar-blue and translucent as it winds and roils past the steep cliffs that look like a Chinese landscape painting. The river's wildness loosens up my culture shock, the silence in the tall coast redwoods settles my soul-collywobbles. By the time I'm on the beach, basalt sea stacks getting pounded by the never-ending waves, I'm back in my body.

Walking the undulating wrack line, three plump beach ravens spotted me. I've always had a soft spot for ravens. They soon determined I was carrying a lunch of sorts. My cheese, crackers, and apple proved an irresistible attraction. They followed me closely. I found a wind-sheltered spot behind a giant greenish stone. The ravens were too cautious to take my tossed offerings but were highly aware I had the goods. They perched and circled, keeping a shiny eye on me. They were so handsome, fine-looking, fit and sleek. I felt gift-love toward them.

I scratched a Valentine's heart in the hard-packed beige sand, near some firs. I wrote "for Raven" inside with a piece of cedar driftwood that smelled of salt and iodine. I set three crackers and an apple core inside.

I felt them moving in on my heart as I strolled down the strand into the stiff south wind. My loves, my Valentines, black and shiny and smart as a whip.

Raven Lives Here

Raven lives here. Raven comes by.

Raven and his wife raise a family each year somewhere up canyon.

In the summer morning he is awake before the songbirds visiting from the south. His feathers are luminous. His feathers are so black they shine blue and silver. Like water.

On short winter afternoons Raven makes his wooden sounds and caws all around this place. He is over there in the madrones. Now at the top of the fir. Raven is proud, but not too proud to look for gifts I leave for him. He takes food for his wife.

In the spring when I am letting the sun shine on my bare back and planting peas, Raven and his wife dance in the sky above my garden. They roll and tumble in an intricate ritual inches apart in the blue openness. They are still in love after all these years. They feel the joy of procreation. They tell each other so. They bless my peas with their love-talk.

In the fall Raven goes missing. He is resting somewhere secret and fasting. At Samhain he seeks his vision for the new year. He stays close to his home up canyon and teaches his children how to live. I miss him then.

Once I saw Raven in the white light of mid-summer high in the sky so that he was small. He was like a mirror reflecting the hard light. He was silver and shining like a star. I like to remember him like that. Silver. A Shining One.

Raven lives here. Raven comes by.

18

Rootedness and Offerings

Feeding self:

It's cool morning and I'm seeking sun, facing straight into the light, red color and brightness bleeding through closed eyelids. I smell the juniper heating up, hear a mountain blue bird pair swoop by.

Words are catching me up. Time goes away. I've been fine tuning meaning all morning. I love the subtle shading and the rabbit-holes of word origin, the sweetness of capturing a moment, or idea, the rare just-rightness that the muse sometimes brings.

I'm walking down-slope toward the muddy river and the long line of cottonwoods growing in the wet zone along the water. It's spring and I catch the honey-resin smell coming from the cottonwood buds.

I'm needle-felting my funeral shroud out of cream-colored wool felt, preparing for my death. I'm weaving a basket out of pine needles, using a long silver needle. I'm wrapping June-collected sage brush into bundles, the smell is like heaven, human catnip.

The winds are really picking up from the northwest. I can feel the wet coming, see the tall thunderheads building on the horizon. Giddy and excited, I listen for the tell-tale rumbling. Everything, everything, is happy and waiting.

I've laid out my morning tarot, look: the Ace of Cups, Temperance, the Magician.

The dark of the moon, and so many stars. Orion's rising and so are the Pleiades. For some reason that part of the sky has always felt like home ground. I feel settled. The great arc of the milky way stretches across the night. I rest on the dusty red earth and almost disappear.

Feeding others:

I make you a gift. It could be bright colored silk or made of stitched hide. Maybe it would be food, hot soup or a berry pie. I put my arm around you. Tell you some story that's meant to make you laugh. Or some story that commiserates.

I offer you a ceremony, sometimes they come to me whole; sometimes I must really work at it. I sing you a song, but oh man, that means I totally trust you, because singing in front of people brings up so much fear.

I sit with you in silence, sharing in the grief that the relentless dissolution of all that seems worthy and alive brings. I show you the bleeding heart clenched on my knees. I look deep into your shrouded eyes and hold therein our mutual sorrow.

I pray for you, think of you, light a candle when you are in a struggle, when you feel sick or you hate your job, or your lover left you.

I write a poem in your honor or share some essays that I've been working on. Take you on a tour to someplace amazing, like Chaco Canyon or Canyon de Chelly or Wupatki. We sit among the hot red rocks and watch the raven's shadow.

I listen without advising. I patch the knee in your favorite jeans.

I collaborate with you on a project or a program. I hug you twelve times in one day.

I find you incredibly valuable. I tell you I love you, that you are beautiful, that I've learned something important from being in your presence.

I make you a gift. I make you a gift because you are one.

19

What I Want My Heart to Be

I want my heart to be a stone, white-hot from the fire, and when the sweetgrass braid touches it a burst of pungent smoke will curl prayers into the sky.

I want my heart to be rising magma, red-hot molten basalt, cracked black on the surface like drying mud flats, a mosaic of directed will and inspiration.

I want my heart to be a lightning strike, electric-blue, fast, sure, fusing sand into glass, transformative, transfiguring, pure as white light.

I want my heart to be a star, as simple as hydrogen, fusing, seven million degrees Kelvin, stable, full of gravitas, joyful in the burning.

20

Thoughts on Climate & Beauty

The growing light wakes me. It slants orangey-pink across the foot of the bed. The light's changed some, rises a tiny bit later with a smidge of southward drift. I need to get up, to do some work. The cat just wants his first breakfast. I shamble, bent over to fit under the ceiling, to the loft edge and crawl down the ladder like a stiff old crab. I'm emerging from my night crevice, my angled place of rest. As I brew my tea, the world rejoins me.

It's still this morning. Not a breeze, not a sound. Even the birds are quiet. I like the silence. I like the smell of juniper. I like the morning light on the red and rust and tan cliffs. I like the lush green and the scattering of colorful blooms in my garden. I like my cat's expectant face. I like caring for him.

I don't know.

Even surrounded by this beauty, even when the hummingbirds come iridescent purple and the sphinx moths flutter at night like ragged ghosts, and Jupiter is shining not far from the Milky Way, I feel lonely. I miss being a wife. I miss the matrix and responsibility of family. I miss the shared quality of experience. Sometimes my heart aches, sore and tight and heavy, acutely aware of what's lost and gone. Lost and gone. Like vapor, things evaporate, phase-change, people come and go, times come and go, places come and go. We aren't built like that. Not really. We're meant, I think, for continuity, for long stretches of things staying the same. Maybe that's my Neanderthal DNA talking. I miss 250,000 years of continuity.

I don't know.

For weeks now, maybe much longer if I consider it, as I go about my business: driving, planning, working, visiting friends, reading, pulses of deep sadness wash over me. I live on the "Verge of Tears", out beyond the pale, a tender territory I seem to occupy more and more. I feel affection, fondness, kind-heartedness, gentleness, compassion, toward *everything*. My darling mice and beetles, oh amazing clouds, the powerful flash of lightning, the raven flying and the pinion pine setting cones. I love this world. I love all the things that have arisen from it. When

I walk the land, I feel ancient magic and elemental power and I sense the dense sweetness of symbiosis. But still the sadness comes. I think, maybe I'm feeling the pain of the Earth, the biosphere, and the ever-escalating pressure is squeezing my heart.

As a society we've been talking about tipping points for decades. As a species we've moved past them I'm afraid. And that's the source of the upwelling sorrow. My heart/soul, a sentient-be-ingness, is super-conscious of the irreversible nature of what we've wrought. I've always carried a cavernous fear of the irreparable, of things that can't be undone, of mistakes that carry the burden of irrevocability, of deadly permanence. It's an on-going deep disenchantment, a true burden, finding that we are truly well over limits, living now on the other side of the ability to make prudent change and *knowing that*. Really knowing it, bone deep. Yet one tries not to cave in to patching that perception over with hope-plasters and rescue-stories. Seeing beautiful Gaia, pushed to unpredictable, elemental, emergent agency and knowing soul deep; that *yes*, we must learn to hunker down, to map a way in an unfamiliar and less friendly world.

We've shaken the sleeping ones, my friends, steepened the angle of repose, let the genie out of the bottle, Pandora from her box. Sometimes my heart aches, sore and tight and heavy, acutely aware of what's lost and gone. Sometimes my heart aches from the fullness, the appreciation for what's here now. What's still whole and working. What's elegant and gorgeous and wild.

The Earth won't die, nature bats last, bacteria rule. It'll all wind up again in a different form. Though there is intense tragedy in losing all the marvelous creations that have been, that are now, I've never bought in to the "end of life on earth" concept. End of life as we know it, yes.

Ironically, humans aren't at risk of extinction. No, *we're weeds*. We'll see our faces along-side starlings and in the trumpets of bindweed for centuries to come. We'll be reflected in the slime of algae blooms and the grins of green iguanas. *We can live suspended over a fucking pit mine*. No, humans won't be going away. *What's going away is comfort and expanding wealth. Biodiversity and stability. Predictability and an easy gift-like abundance.* The rich will have their enclaves and the poor will scrabble. No end in sight, no end at all.

I keep busy. I make lists every day and I work hard. I join committees and build up the soil in my gardens. I try like the devil to be kind. I used to think I had something to teach, but I find I'm only hungry to learn. I love people who are honest and do their best to speak truth. I love people who are working on implementing great ideas or making art or trying to help (somewhere, something) or who listen to their dream-world for direction. I love animals and plants and stars. I love the strength of my ancestors and the watery places we came from and I love my child and the places I've been diaspora-ed to. I yearn for a sweet healthy planet for our progeny.

Like I said, I work hard. I'm tired at the end of each day. I like to pretend I have a purpose.

I've thought about this all day, how I feel about what's happening. I hear the urgency and pain and confusion in so many of the voices that I love. I feel it too. The anxiety-over-the-state-of-the-world is ever-present, vague, distressing, and free-floating. Today, I've tried to express how I experience our crazily chaotic spinning world. To express to you what it means to me when I read, "we have about 18 months," instead of that lovely projected decade, to change direction on our juggernaut-wild-ride-to-uncertainty. To express what it means to be alive right now and part of a lineage, a culture, a species. To wonder how families come apart and to think about our inability to do reparations *even at that scale*. To feel the immense loneliness of being human and to still get up and make that second cup of tea and go work in the studio.

The light is fading. It's still quiet. The cat has had his second supper. As I crab-shimmy back up my loft ladder to crawl into my angular crevice for rest, I look lovingly at my companion-cat. He curls up to sleep, blissfully in the moment. I don't think he worries, except about first breakfast and second supper. I would like that kind of respite from the forethought of grief. (dear Wendell Berry) I feel the breeze pick up and watch the thunderheads build, smell the juniper and dust, I hear a cricket start to sing, and I feel sadness and gratitude in equal measure.

So, what to do?

I don't know.

Maybe this is all happening to make us feel the love sharply, sense our interdependence keenly, and to see the lines of separation as the fictious fractures they are. To make us grieve the losses, atone for the excesses, propitiate the wild gods, and cast a larger circle of protection. I learned a new word from Martin Shaw, who knows a TON of amazing words. *Apotropaic.* The definition is: having the power to avert evil influences or bad luck.

I want that protection. For all of us.

About the Author

Susan Cross lives in northern New Mexico, well-wisher to ravens, bears, bumblebees, rattlesnakes and coyotes. She works from her tiny house on a windy mesa above the Rio Puerco canyon as a craftsperson, ceremonialist, and Jill-of-all-trades. She's a burial shroud maker, rawhide hand drum and rattle builder, a ceremony writer, a gardener, an *old* mother, a tour driver, a grief-stricken naturalist drowning her sorrows with single malt scotch, and a weary-but-wonder-filled pilgrim. She strives to remain a humble student in the school of hard knocks.

Susan has felt called in recent decades by the deep past which has led her on sojourns to many Neolithic and Bronze Age sites in the landscapes of her people, to ancestral healing, and trying to understand the strange impacts of diaspora. She's exploring ways to "preserve the archaic whisper" by seeking strategies to safeguard pieces of our humanity that are at on-going risk of atrophy.

Susan Cross
Soaring Raven Services
PO Box 1133
Abiquiu, New Mexico 87510
520-248-9938
www.soaringravenservices.com
www.etsy.com/shop/SoaringRavenStore
Follow on Instagram: soaringravenservicessusancross

Made in the USA
Columbia, SC
25 November 2020